Coaching Tools

Coaching Tools

101 coaching tools and techniques for executive coaches, team coaches, mentors and supervisors: WeCoach! Volume 2

Edited by

Jonathan Passmore, Claudia Day, Julie Flower,

Maggie Grieve and Jelena Jovanovic Moon

First published in 2022 by Libri Publishing

Copyright © Libri Publishing

The right of Jonathan Passmore, Claudia Day, Julie Flower, Maggie Grieve and Jelena Jovanovic Moon to be identified as the editors of this work has been asserted in accordance with the Copyright, Designs and Patents Act, 1988.

ISBN 978-1-911450-89-4

A CIP catalogue record for this book is available from The British Library

Cover and Design by Carnegie Book Production
Cover graphic by Mina Krstajic

Printed in the UK by Halstan

Libri Publishing
Brunel House
Volunteer Way
Faringdon
Oxfordshire
SN7 7YR

Tel: +44 (0)845 873 3837

www.libripublishing.co.uk

Contents

Contributors

Badri Bajaj

Magdalena Bak-Maier

Iona Boniwell

Calum Byers

Paul Crick

Claudia Day

Jonathan Drew

Eversley Felix

Claire Finch

Julie Flower

Karen Foy

Johan Frederik Banzhaf

Taff Gidi

Suzy Green

Maggie Grieve

Suzanne Hayes-Jones

Marc Innegraeve

Yannick Jacob

Jelena Jovanovic Moon

Aidan Kerr

Christine Lithgow Smith

Nicholas Lord

David Love

Deb McEwen

Kaveh Mir

Tia Moin

Fiona Moore

Neil Munz-Jones

Callum O'Neill

Adeola Oludemi

Rebecca Palmer

Naeema Pasha

Jonathan Passmore

Harriet Pemberton

Sarah Perrott

Mike Phillips

Alex Porter

Pirjo Puhakka

Theresa Quinn

Claire Rason

Sabine Renner

Viki Rice

Clare Richards

Matt Richards

Pippa Ruxton

Clare Smale

Mark Smith

Wendy-Ann Smith

Phil Summerfield

Christian van Nieuwerburgh

Jacqui Zanetti

The Editors

Maggie Grieve

Maggie is a leadership and team coach with 30 years of board level strategy, partnering and business development experience. She left her Global Partnering Strategy Director role with BT Plc in 2016, to start Ping Thinking, where she pursues her combined passions of people and strategy, by helping businesses, teams and individuals create meaningful, structured and supported change, with an emphasis on recognition, appreciation and utilisation of their own strengths and resources. Maggie holds professional qualifications in Executive (Henley) and Team (WBECS) Coaching, a business degree (BA) and marketing Diploma (CIM) and is an accredited EMCC Team Coach, AC Professional Coach and Lumina Psychometrics Practitioner.

Maggie Grieve

Jonathan Passmore

Jonathan is Senior VP Coaching at CoachHub, the digital coaching platform, and director of the Henley Centre for Coaching, Henley Business School. He is an accredited executive coach, supervisor and chartered psychologist. He has published widely with over 30 books on coaching, leadership, change and mindfulness, including *Becoming a Coach: The Essential ICF Guide* and *The Coaches' Handbook*. He has also published over 100 scientific papers and book chapters, and his work has been recognised with multiple awards from professional bodies including the British Psychological Society, Association of Business Psychologists and EMCC.

Jonathan Passmore

Julie Flower

Julie Flower is a leadership development consultant, facilitator and coach who focuses on positive social change impact in complex systems. She holds an MSc in Coaching and Behavioural Change and is an external tutor in executive coaching at Henley Business School. With senior experience in the public, private and non-profit sectors, Julie leads The Specialist Generalist, a learning and development practice. She is also an improvised comedy performer and integrates learning from improv with other evidence-based behavioural change approaches to help leaders and teams navigate uncertainty.

Julie Flower

Claudia Day

Claudia is a back-to-work coach, who after starting her family and working in multiple roles and industries across the globe – including in cancer research, management consulting, NGOs, and customer retention – appreciated how difficult change can be. This motivated her to venture into the industry. Claudia holds professional qualifications in Executive Coaching from Henley Business School, an MBA from MIT Sloan School of Management and is accredited by EMCC. She is also an entrepreneur, starting eHuddle (an online coaching platform designed to provide coaches with an end-to-end solution that covers admin, development and remote coaching).

Claudia Day

Jelena Jovanovic Moon

Jelena is a psychologist with degrees in coaching and organisational change from Henley Business School and people management from LSE. Holding senior leadership and consulting roles in people management and organisational development across private, public and non-profit sectors, she has supported organisations through fast growth and people in embracing change. This is where she discovered her passion for coaching, as any successful change starts with a lightbulb moment in someone's mind. Now through coaching she is driven to switch on as many lightbulbs as possible.

Jelena Jovanovic Moon

Acknowledgements from the Editors

We are deeply grateful to everybody who has inspired, supported and collaborated with us to create these Coaching Tools books! *WeCoach!* has certainly been an ambitious project and we would like to offer a few personal acknowledgements to those who have made this possible.

First of all, huge thanks are due to our wonderful contributors, all of whom have generously taken the time to share their knowledge and expertise with a wider community, allowing the creation of books with a compilation of their favourite tools. The tools and approaches in this book and its sister book, Volume 2, reflect the diversity of backgrounds and experience of our contributors, who include world leaders in coaching, behavioural change practitioners and managers and leaders from a wide range of sectors. The books are a labour of love and we have, on everybody's behalf, a feeling of enormous achievement.

We should also mention the truly vibrant learning community that is The Henley Centre for Coaching at Henley Business School, which has been at the heart of this adventure. The Centre creates connections and a community like no other. We hope that our books make some contribution to sharing the very best in coaching worldwide.

There have been many 'What are we doing?' moments, as well as moments of angst, joy, elation, exhaustion and everything in between. As editors, passionate about coaching, we've been fully fuelled to work as a hub of top-notch collaboration. We would like to acknowledge and appreciate the unique skills and way of being that we have each brought to the team:

- Jonathan, his ambition, guidance and energy, without which we'd have sunk this ship a long time ago! Indeed, without his incredible commitment, helping us to navigate our way, the book might never have even left harbour.
- Jelena, her dry humour a valuable safety valve, always there to save the day, bravely and repeatedly diving into an agitated spreadsheet sea, calmly creating a miracle of order from chaos.
- Claudia, somehow managing the many thrashing tentacles of our financial model, keeping us true and aligned to the self-funded and collaborative ethos of the project – no mean fight and feat!
- Julie, our very own diplomat, calm in every storm and an expert, yet professional cowboy with an astounding ability to corral us when we strayed from the ranch.
- Maggie, with unbounded vitality levels, taking on whatever was needed to keep the ignition on and the project going; when we were all out of energy, she came with vigour and kept us in motion.

Special thanks also go to Celia Cozens and the whole team at Libri who believed in us and created a publishing model for something that had never been done before in the coaching world. Thank you for your ambition, good humour and patience, as we brought together so many different strands.

Finally, we'd like to say a few words of personal thanks:

Claudia

To my family and friends for being so supportive, and giving me unconditional love during those weekends of work. To my clients, for allowing me to work in a field I love. And to my fellow editors for making this experience amazing.

Julie

To my friends, family, clients and colleagues (past, present and future), who inspire, delight, challenge and teach me every day. To my fellow editors, for an incredible experience of teamwork. And to my mum, for the joy you brought.

Maggie

To my daughters and husband, my family and very dear friends – your support is bountiful, generous and so deeply appreciated. To my clients, my inspiration to keep learning and challenging the art of the possible. And to my amazing co-editors – the best tigers ever!

Jelena

To all people I was fortunate to coach, for their trust and inspiration. To my dear family, for always being there and teaching me that everything is possible. To my fellow editors, for making this journey one of the best team-work experiences, resulting not only in a valuable book, but also in new friendships for life.

Jonathan

To the global coach community, who are helping leaders and managers all over the globe, change the world one conversation at a time.

Introduction

'Individually, we are one drop. Together, we are an ocean.'– Ryunosuke Satoro

Something amazing happens when people invest and work towards the same goal – things change. Our *Coaching Tools* books – a collaborative effort, that draws together coaches from around the world to share their favourite practices – are living evidence of that. The result is, we hope, the richest collection of coaching tools and techniques ever compiled, providing coaching professionals with a wonderful resource.

Before you read Volume 2, perhaps you'd like to hear a little about the background of why we created the books and how they are different from any other coaching books. For a group of experienced coaches and business leaders, enrolled on the MSc in Coaching and Behavioural Change at Henley Business School, the pressure was on. A submission deadline loomed, and supportive advice and encouragement flowed in ever-increasing quantities between group members. A seemingly innocent question suddenly stopped us all dead in our tracks: 'Can anyone recommend a good coaching techniques and tools book?' A simple question for a group awash with coaching experience. Surely a river of suggestions would instantly flow. But what happened was a moment's silence, as we all stopped to think. Of course, after a while, some suggestions emerged, but what remained was a realisation that despite our tremendous combined experience, none of us had a 'best' coaching book that we could suggest for capable, professional coaches to turn to, for a wide variety of evidence-based coaching tools and techniques. The question lingered and caused the group to consider how we might change this. Four of us volunteered to champion the idea and before too long, we garnered support from our Henley Professor, Jonathan Passmore, who also saw the potential.

Together, we embarked on exploring and developing the idea further.

Thoughts emerged on how a resource like this, with tried-and-tested methodology at its heart, provided in a highly visual, easy to read, inviting to browse through and reflect on format, could really help coaches to prepare for exceptional client sessions. We reached out across the Henley network and collected a large handful of coaches' great favourites – our initial aim was for 50. The enthusiasm and momentum increased as our 'best of the best' concept gained visibility in the wider professional coaching community and before we knew it our 50 had become over 200. The project, now known as *WeCoach!*, continued to expand, and with it came enthusiastic contributions from those at the very top of our field: exciting! Something very special and new had been created – a full and wholesome collection of favourite tools from an exceptional group of coaches, ready to be shared with the worldwide coaching community.

Our excitement and achievement gained the attention of our proposed publishers and now our idea looked like it could become a reality. This story is at the very heart of the volume you now hold in your hands – a collaboration and contribution of tried-and-tested personal favourites from amongst the very best in our field provided as an easy to use, rich source of applied tools and techniques that had hitherto not existed. All of this could never have been achieved without the valuable contributions and support of the 90+ fellow coaches who helped create these books and for this we thank them all. It is this that changed our single 'drop' of an idea into an 'ocean' of joint achievement.

During the process, we decided to make the books stand out from anything that had been produced before. First for the diversity and the scale of contributions and contributors to create an acknowledged go-to resource with 200+ tools and two volumes.

Second for the eclectic nature of the tools, reflecting the range of contributors, drawing disparately from Behavioural, Cognitive Behavioural, Motivational Interviewing, Acceptance and Commitment Therapy, Compassion, Positive Psychology, Psychodynamic, Gestalt, Solution-focused, Mindfulness and Neuroscience frameworks amongst others.

Third, inspired by the idea of the accessibility and usefulness of a really good recipe book, we decided to present the books in an easy-to-use design with each tool simple to find, containing clear ingredients, a description and a step-by-step method. Of course, coaching is not cooking. The coach needs to decide which, if any, tool to use with a client, and how to introduce it. Whilst the presentation is common across the tools and simple in its structure, we hope that coaches will add them to their repertoire and adapt them in unique ways to ensure each client is respected for the unique and wonderful creation they are.

The final ambition for the books that struck fear into many of the publishers we approached, was our decision to publish colour books, rich with images to inspire coaches in their work – useful and beautiful in equal measure.

Thankfully, our publisher Libri also understood how all these elements combined to provide something with great potential for professional coaches and so, the collection and the presentation became a reality.

Turning our idea into books has absolutely been as hard as it sounds, but the reward of creating a resource that supports the global coach community to help leaders, managers, and people all over the world has made every minute of effort worthwhile. So, the next time someone blithely asks the question 'can anyone recommend…' we hope there will be no silence and you will offer them our WeCoach! *Coaching Tools* books as the very best resource of coaching tools, methods and techniques, knowledge and wisdom available.

What is a coaching tool?

During coach training and as you progress through your career, you are likely to draw on a range of theoretical approaches and pick up a sometimes dizzying array of tools and techniques. It may seem that each new development module or learning workshop you attend presents yet more handy diagrams, acronyms and models. As coaches, we believe in an evidence-based but diverse approach, which includes tools, techniques, models and exercises that experienced contributors have found useful in their coaching work with clients.

Tools, by definition, are helpful when focused on a particular job. The skill of the coach is to identify when one of these may be useful, to support a client with a particular situation, issue or aim. The tools are drawn from a range of different coaching approaches (such as cognitive behavioural, humanistic and Gestalt) and other disciplines as diverse as leadership and management theory and improvised comedy. They include questioning techniques, visual models, practical frameworks and some very creative approaches. All can help to bring structure and focus to your coaching conversations. We hope that they will provide inspiration and food for thought and find practical application in your work.

They are intended to be used, adapted and integrated into your wider coaching practice, within the bounds of your own professional competence, preference and curiosity. You will amplify the use of the tools through the quality of your questions, your presence and your knowledge of underpinning coaching theory and the evidence around behavioural change. They are presented in an easy-to-follow 'recipe' format but are not intended to bring a formulaic approach to coaching. Many of the tools can be used equally well in individual and group or team coaching settings. It is hoped that you will find something in here to add to your existing repertoire of tools and techniques, in order to best support your clients.

A tool is only a tool and can never replace a strong client relationship, a sound theoretical base or core coaching skills. Both Hardingham (2006) and Passmore (2007) advocate an 'eclectic' approach that synthesises tools, techniques and frameworks from a range of approaches through their respective British Eclectic and Integrated Coaching models. The emphasis remains on the client, the relationship and the context. However, coaching tools can provide clients with new and helpful ways of exploring situations, reflecting and structuring their thoughts, as well as gaining commitment to act. They can also provide a refreshing change in energy and different way of working, for both client and coach.

References

Hardingham, A. (2006) The British Eclectic Model of Coaching: Towards Professionalism without Dogma. *International Journal of Mentoring and Coaching*, IV (1), 11–14.

Passmore, J. (2007) An Integrated Model for Executive Coaching. *Consulting Psychology Journal*, 59(1), 68–78.

How to introduce tools to clients

In deciding which tool to use, coaches should follow their experience and wisdom (Wilson, 2014, p.222). As an integrated coach drawing on a range of models, your focus will be to select a tool based on your client and their presenting issue, as well as taking into account your own training and strengths (Passmore, 2021).

As coaches, we know the potential tools have to help clients to move on when stuck, to develop fresh thinking or to create new insights. But for the client, any tool we offer is likely to be new to them. Some clients may have had negative experiences with something similar, for example being told that they cannot draw, leading to a reluctance to step out of the comfort zone or traditional ways of working, for example if invited to play with Lego or go for a coaching walk.

It is important to keep in mind the risks when introducing a tool:
- The client might not like the tool, or feel uncomfortable with it.
- The client might not engage with the tool, for instance, if they feel fear that it might reveal something they are not ready to handle, or because they have no faith in it being effective.
- The tool may not have the impact the coach expects, and it may not move the client forward or generate new awareness.
- It might break rapport.
- The tool may challenge the skills of the client.
- The tool may be difficult to execute with the resources available (e.g. physical space).
- The tool may be subjected to perceptions that the client holds of how things are and should be.

Taking into consideration all of the above, when introducing a tool, the coach needs to make sure they do it in a way that avoids these risks.

Eight guiding principles

1. **Choice**: Choose the tool based on the client's needs and not your personal agenda.
2. **Rapport**: Make sure rapport is strong. If rapport is broken at the early stages of the relationship, it may be more difficult to build it again than if there is a strong relationship already (Hardingham, 2004).
3. **Time:** Be aware how long you have in the session. Some tools can be introduced without any explanation, some are short, maybe less than a minute, while others may take the whole coaching session.
4. **Consent:** Ask for permission: "Would you be comfortable if we did something a little different?"
5. **Explain**: Give background about the tool, an overview of how it has been used in the past and how it could be helpful in this case.
6. **Options**: Give the client options. The driver of the coaching relationship is the client: they always have the option to give the tool a try – or not.
7. **Experiment**: Explain that it is an 'experiment' – and just see how it goes. This gives you and them the right for the experiment to 'fail', with no pressure or expectation on either side.
8. **Reflect:** Reflect on how it went, both with the client and on your own, to learn from the experience and use it in future sessions.

While tools can add to our work with clients, they need to be introduced sensitively and tactfully, respecting each individual and the issues they bring.

References

Wilson, C. (2014) *Performance Coaching: A Complete Guide to Best Practice Coaching and Training* (2nd edition). London: Kogan Page.

Hardingham, A. (2004) *The Coach's Coach*. London: Chartered Institute of Personnel and Development.

Passmore, J. (2021) Developing an Integrated Coaching Approach. In Passmore, J., *The Coaches' Handbook: The Complete Practitioner Guide for Professional Coaches*. Abingdon: Routledge, pp.322–330.

Five Alternative Uses For

Ingredients

An object or objects (anything will do)

When does it work best?

This versatile and fun exercise can help when clients want to think more flexibly and creatively. It can be a very useful warm-up exercise before more traditional or focused creative problem-solving. As it is a very simple and portable exercise, it can be done spontaneously and with minimal resources. Some clients may feel they respond particularly well to the use of a physical object in terms of accessing ideas.

Julie Flower is a leadership and team development coach, consultant and facilitator, specialising in navigating uncertainty in complex systems and applied improvisation.

Description

This is a very simple exercise that puts a client on the spot by asking them to rapidly describe five alternative uses for an everyday object. It is drawn from improvised comedy and is designed to encourage spontaneity, creativity and flexibility of thinking. It also encourages us to challenge our assumptions about the everyday by considering other possibilities. By making this a rapid exercise, clients do not have time to filter or appraise their ideas to come up with the 'correct' or 'best' answer.

Step by step

1. Invite the client to select an object from their environment. It may help to choose something slightly unusual or with moving parts but this isn't essential.
2. Offer a couple of minutes of guided exploration of the object, building their attention. Encourage them to explore the size, shape, weight, texture, sound and other properties of the object.
3. Ask them to rapidly reel off five alternative uses for the object. The ideas do not have to be in the realm of the 'realistic' or 'feasible' but should be as specific as possible (i.e. "as a grooming implement for a squirrel" rather than "as a piece of modern art").
4. Show your appreciation for the ideas and encourage a discussion about how it felt to be put on the spot, what tactics the client used to come up with ideas, and how the principles could apply in their work or wider life.
5. It may be helpful to repeat the exercise a number of times with different objects. A further development would be to ask them to apply the same 'five alternative uses for' principles to a challenge at work as a rapid-fire solution-generating exercise.
6. Close the exercise by inviting them to think about that process and how the insights might apply to their current issue.

Floating Team Sculpt

Ingredients

A room with everyday objects in it – or with some extra random objects added by the coach

Description

Peter Hawkins developed the theme of the Jacob Moreno sociodrama to help explore, in an experiential way, the underlying dynamics of teams (Moreno and Toeman, 1942). Hawkins uses the term 'floating' because no one person is doing the sculpting and the sculpt is the product of the emerging team dynamic.

Step by step

1. The coach asks the team to look around and find objects and/or symbols that represent in some way how they think of what's at the heart or core of the team. They are then asked to place these in the middle of the room.
2. The team members are not allowed to discuss this and are asked then to stand up and move around the room to find a place within the room that symbolises to them where they feel they are within the assembled group. The coach can add further explanation or ask questions such as who are they close to, who are they far away from and how far away are they from the middle?
3. Next, they are asked to create a pose that encapsulates how they are in the group. This can take a few moments, because each person's move is affected by other people's moves. It's important to wait/give enough time for everyone to be comfortable with their chosen position.
4. Next, each person is asked to make a statement about how they feel about that position: it should start with "In this position in the team, I feel…".
5. Each team member is given the opportunity to explore how they would like to move to a different position in the team. They are asked to describe what that move requires for them and for the others inside and outside the group. An example of this could be that one person would like to be closer to the centre – they can be asked to describe how they would find their way there and then to describe what the move would feel like both for themselves and for others.
6. The next step offers an opportunity for all team members to explore the team in a different context. To do this, they are all asked to consider thinking of the team in a different situation. Hawkins suggests asking, for example, "if this team were a family, what sort of family would it be? Who would be in what role?" Or "If this team were a television programme, which programme would it be? Who would be in what role and what would be happening between the people – the transactions between them?" Other possibilities suggested by Hawkins include meals, animals, countries, modes of transport, myths and Shakespearean plays (Hawkins, 2017). You can pick any situation you like to help the team think outside of their usual frame of reference.

When does it work best?

This works well with an established team or with teams of people who work together as part of their usual engagement in their roles. It allows every team member to become physically involved in the discussion because it uses their very presence to help to illustrate the underlying dynamics of the group(s). As well as creating a sense of inclusivity, it has the potential to increase the value that each member contributes to, and receives from, the team.

Floating Team Sculpt

7. Finally, work with the team members to offer them a chance to leave their positions to stand on a chair and look at the structure that's been created by and with the other team members. Then describe to them that, by standing on this chair, they hold the lead as Creative Coach to the team. Encourage them to tell the team in a simple statement what they would encourage or discourage the team to do. You can give them a standard sentence to make this statement such as "if I were coach to this team, I would…". Hawkins suggests that the Creative Coaches on the chair should be encouraged not to think or share what they would say until they actually stand on the chair so their immediate take on their observations can be captured.

References

Hawkins, P. (2017) *Leadership Team Coaching, Developing Transformational Leadership* (3rd edition). London: Kogan Page.

Moreno, J.L., and Toeman, Z. (1942) The Group Approach in Psychodrama. *Sociometry*, 5, 191–194. https://doi.org/10.2307/2785432

Maggie Grieve combines 30 years of global business-development leadership experience, team and executive coaching accreditations and her passion for facilitating lasting, positive change to help individuals and teams succeed and be happy in life and business.

Gift-giving Tree

Ingredients

A comfortable, relaxed environment

When does it work best?

The technique works best when the client is feeling stuck and needs inspiration. They may be unable to see that they have inner strengths. By opening up this possibility, the client can discover a strength, use it in their coaching challenge, and generally feel more positive about moving forward. It is vital that a good rapport has been established as the client needs to feel comfortable with their eyes closed.

Description

The 'Gift-giving Tree' is a yoga visualisation technique used to uncover a strength that the client has hidden within their subconscious mind. This strength can then be applied to a coaching challenge. The visualisation begins in nature, experiencing the five senses. This phase should not be rushed, as it supports the next phase when choosing a gift from the Gift-giving Tree. The chosen gift represents a hidden strength that the client already has.

It is important that the client describes their gift in detail, using all five senses if possible. The coach's role is to notice the client's description and listen for repeating phrases or non-verbal clues that can be explored further. Take care not to make assumptions or judgements about the meaning of the gift for the client, and avoid any unconscious reactions. For example, the gift of a book may represent knowledge to one client, but something entirely different to another. Once the hidden strength has been uncovered, it can be brought into this or a future coaching session.

Step by step

1. Explain the model to the client in the coaching session.
2. Ask the client to sit comfortably and close their eyes.
3. Invite the client to take three slow, deep breaths, in through their nose and out through their mouth, and then return to normal breathing.
4. Ask the client to focus on the space in front of their closed eyes.
5. You will now guide the client through a visualisation, asking the client to:
   i. Imagine they are walking along a path in nature (at this point, you may wish to close your own eyes, as this can help set the right pace);
   ii. Slowly notice in turn the sights, sounds, smells, tastes and feel of things around them (you can suggest trees, flowers, birds, insects, fruit, cool water from a stream, soft grass, gentle breeze, etc.);
   iii. Observe a tree set apart in the near distance, and walk towards it; this is the Gift-giving Tree;
   iv. Notice that there are gifts hanging in the tree; reach up and take one that you are drawn to;
   v. Sit on a nearby bench and open the gift; describe it out loud in as much detail as possible (e.g. size, shape, colour, smell, sound, how it feels to touch, etc.);
   vi. Think about what the gift means to them.
6. Ask the client to return to the coaching room in their mind when they are ready, bringing their gift with them. Then they can slowly open their eyes.
7. Discuss the gift with the client, asking them to describe it and what it means to them.
8. Focus on any repeated words or phrases and explore these in more depth.

Gift-giving Tree

9. Take care not to make assumptions or judgements about the meaning of the gift for the client, and avoid any unconscious reactions.
10. Suggest to the client that the gift represents a strength that they already have.
11. Discuss with the client how this strength could be applied to their coaching challenge.

Clare Richards is a PCC-accredited Henley coach and yoga teacher.

Future Me Letter

Ingredients

Paper (ideally letter paper)

Envelope

Pen

When does it work best?

This tool is most helpful when the client is facing a challenging and emotional decision (van Nieuwerburgh, 2014). It might be something more tangible like getting a new job, saving money, or getting to an ideal weight or state of health. It could also be something not quite so measurable, such as gaining confidence. The letter writing allows the person to think forwards to a time when the decision will have been taken, and the length of time provides distance from the situation so that they may view it from a more detached perspective.

Description

The client is asked to write a letter to themself from a date in the future – this could be 10 years, 20 years, etc. In the letter, the client will be writing to themselves from the future and giving advice about how to manage the situation they are in. By looking into the future using a solution-focused approach, the client is 'forced' to consider medium or longer term goals in a way that taps into their knowledge and personal expertise of themselves. This enables clients to build on existing strengths and abilities.

Step by step

1. Ask the client to assume that they have reached their described goal and that they are going to write a letter back to themselves.
2. Tell them that they should write the date on the letter, start with a greeting to themselves and conclude with a signature from themselves too. Reassure the client that the letter is entirely confidential and that no-one needs to know what is in it – even you, as coach. The letter can be written during the coaching session. You can stay in the room or leave the client to write it alone. You can also suggest the client writes the letter as homework between sessions.
3. Tell the client that they should think about including giving themselves the good advice and encouragement that they might give to someone else.
4. Although you will not ask the client to read the letter aloud, you can still ask if there was any interesting advice in the letter and discuss this further, if it is helpful to do so (see step 6).
5. Give the client the envelope and suggest that it is their choice to keep the letter or lock it away and read it when the time it is written from comes.
6. Ask the client whether the letter contained any useful ideas. Also ask how helpful the letter writing activity was.

Reference

van Nieuwerburgh, C. (2014) *An Introduction to Coaching Skills, A Practical Guide.* London: Sage.

Maggie Grieve combines 30 years of global business-development leadership experience, team and executive coaching accreditations and her passion for facilitating lasting, positive change to help individuals and teams succeed and be happy in life and business.

Grid™ Coaching – Personal and Professional Empowerment and Effectiveness

Ingredients

Paper or flipchart

Pens or markers

Two pieces of rope or string (if working in an embodied way)

Description

Grid™ is a visual, creative and systemic coaching tool. It sorts all activities into four areas called quadrants: (1) life, (2) self-care, (3) work and (4) career (see diagram). It then applies several key principles – clarification, organisation, balance, energy management, inter-relatedness, account-ability, and the importance of completion as well as integration of the big picture with daily activity. It helps the user clarify, map and realise their aspirations, creating results in balance with life, instead of at the expense of it.

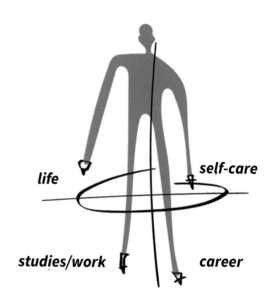

When does it work best?

Grid™ will suit clients who wish to:
- Improve their productivity and wellbeing
- Balance their varied roles and commitments with flare
- Alleviate stress and overwhelm from too much work
- Stop suffering from work–life balance issues
- End self-sabotage
- Heal from burnout
- Make quick progress and achieve tangible results
- Discover a path into a personally resonant purpose and leadership style.

Step by step

With Grid™ coaching, you can really explore your creativity as a coach. Below is one pathway to try.
1. **Introducing the Grid™ to the client**. In this step we bring the tool to serve the client's coaching agenda.
2. **Grid™ set up**. Using either paper or the floor, we recreate the four-quadrant Grid™ set up and explore boundaries between the different

*Grid™ Coaching
– Personal and
Professional
Empowerment
and
Effectiveness*

References

Bak-Maier, M. (2012) *Get Productive! Boosting Your Productivity and Getting Things Done*. Capstone.

Bak-Maier, M. (2015) *The Get Productive Grid: A Simple and Proven Work–Life Balance System to Help You Thrive*. Make Time Count Ltd.

Bak-Maier, M. (2019) *The Grid™ Unlocked*, 14(4), pp.48–51. Available from: https://www.coaching-at-work.com

Dr Magdalena Bak-Maier is an international teacher who helps people reconnect with their full potential.

sections. We can also invite the client to imagine or step into each area to explore what it's like to be there and how they would like it to feel once things improve.

3. **Exploring what's already working**. Using Appreciative Inquiry, we invite the client to notice what already exists in each quadrant that is good, that works and which the client is grateful for. We can deepen this inquiry into emotional and somatic sensations by asking questions such as *"Tell me how this makes you feel?"* or *"What key emotions arise as you experience yourself in this area?"*

4. **Setting goals**. We can establish key goals for the Grid™ overall and/or for specific quadrants. For example, a client may wish to work on their career or their personal or work relationships.

5. **Exploring key imbalances and conflicts**. Grid™ easily highlights any dominance of specific quadrants or particular scarcities. While clients may come into coaching already aware of such imbalances, exploring them in greater depth in the coaching sessions often illuminates key levers of behaviour change needed to help the client meet their needs and aspirations.

6. **Coaching key issues to allow the desired solution to emerge**. Here, we explore a specific issue through the Grid™ lens. This may include locating the issue to a specific quadrant, exploring key beliefs, values and assumptions, associated emotions and the impact of these on real and desired behaviours, as well as key stakeholders. Working within the whole framework also helps reveal how an issue in one area may also pop up elsewhere. Such realisations are often incredibly powerful for the client.

7. **Testing resolve and forward-pacing action**. Grid™ offers a very clear structure where all activities are clustered by theme. This means that when specific actions are identified, they can be tested in terms of: (a) the client's natural orientation towards or away from the action, and (b) helping the client notice the impact of a specific action on everything else.

8. **Closing the session with gratitude and a personally strengthening claim**. To close the session, we invite the client to affirm something specific in each quadrant or for the Grid™ as a whole. A coach may also ask the client to make a strengthening claim towards him- or herself and/or the specific Grid™ quadrant. For example:
    *   "I serve this work"
    *   "This is my need and I have a right to it"
    *   "I love my family/partner/child as they are"
    *   "My purpose is to serve women with my work."

9. **Short debrief with client**. Here, we give space for the client to integrate their learning and what's different for them.

10. **Note taking and further self-development**. For coaches new and seasoned, I recommend making brief notes on sessions.

Hot-air Balloon – for Individuals and Teams

Ingredients

Large piece of paper

Post-it notes

Pens

When does it work best?

In one-to-one coaching, it is most helpful when the client has multiple factors to consider in making a choice, but is struggling to identify and prior- itise them – for example, when making a career decision, or relationship or location choices. For team or organi- sational coaching, it can be used to help teams visualise their current reality and prioritise what is required to take them forward, as a team. It has the power to unite the team around a goal or to help reach a consensus on their reality, as well as helping all team members to think differently and collectively as a team.

Description

The 'Hot-air Balloon' uses the image of a hot-air balloon and weights/ballast as a means of visualising priorities where a client is facing a complex decision. Similarly, the image of the hot-air balloon can be used with teams – leadership or operational – to help gain clarity around what is working well and what is weighing the team down. For both, it is a powerful metaphor and tool to help individuals and teams think about situations in a different way.

Step by step (one-to-one coaching)

1. Invite the client to write down their wish list as it relates to the specific situation or objective they wish to discuss (e.g. a new business, new role or life decision). Each wish should be written on a separate Post-it note. Encourage them to allow enough thinking time for this. Do not rush them and make much use of the "and what else?" question to tease out the wishes that they may feel more reticent to share or feel confident about.
2. Using the large piece of paper or whiteboard, draw a hot-air balloon, with a large basket.
3. The Post-it notes then become individual weights hanging on the side of the basket. Ask the client to stick these on to the balloon diagram.
4. Ask the client to imagine that the balloon has sprung a slow leak. One of the weights will have to be cut loose. Which can they afford to drop?
5. The item selected is removed and recorded elsewhere as the lowest priority from the list. One by one, the weights are allowed to fall, using this same process with the client, until only one is left.
6. Review the now prioritised Post-its with the client. How does the client feel about the resulting priority rankings?
7. Any hints that the client had difficulty in letting go of any of the weights can be useful to explore together.

Step by step (team coaching)

1. Using a large piece of paper or a whiteboard that is visible to all, draw a picture of a hot-air balloon, with ballast bags over the sides and people in the basket, approaching a mountain side. Draw some trees at the base of the mountain side. Next to the balloon basket, draw a large down arrow and next to it write "keeping us down". Next to the balloon itself, draw a large down arrow and write "keeping us up". Against the mountain side, write "risks/concerns".
2. As you draw, explain the concept of what you are about to embark on together by describing the scene and asking them to imagine that they, as a team, are in the hot-air balloon to enjoy the gorgeous landscape on a beautiful sunny day. Ask them questions as you do this, such as "what

Hot-air Balloon – for Individuals and Teams

will happen if there is too much weight attached to the basket?" "What do you think the impact of the size of the balloon and the quality of the burner is?" and so on. This should generate discussion around the need for a good burner and a balloon size that keeps them in the air, as well as highlighting the impact of unnecessary ballast working against them, weighing them down. It will also set the scene of the team as one, making decisions together that impact them all.

3. Suggest that you use this image together to see how it relates to them as a team in terms of their relationships, people, processes, tools, and what they offer as an organisation to clients.

4. Ask them individually, or in pairs, to write on the Post-it notes for the three aspects of:
   a. What is Keeping us Up?
   b. What is Keeping us Down?
   c. What are our Risks/Concerns?

5. Then ask them to take turns to put their notes in the respective areas on the picture. As they take their turn, ask them to briefly explain their notes and encourage the rest of the team to ask questions to clarify or to add any thoughts they have regarding the points made.

6. Once this has been completed, ask the team to group similar Post-its together. Generate further discussion around this with further challenging questions that help to tease out what this means for team members, and for the team's and the organisation's goals, clients and so on. As you do this, try to draw them back to the big picture of the whole scene and how the elements work together, as well as allowing them to describe some of the detail. To help this process, you may opt also to share your own reflections to generate further discussion, although this will depend on the dynamics of your group.

7. You may then ask the team to identify and agree on one or two particular improvement areas for the 'Keeping us Down' and the 'Risks/Concerns' categories. You could ask team members in turn to approach the picture and place a dot against their preferred area to achieve this. As areas are selected, again explore the impact of these decisions by encouraging questions around the impact of these decisions on the team goal and purpose. What will it mean for the organisation, the teams and other stakeholders – clients and suppliers?

8. The team can then agree to create a plan for these selected areas in a further session. Ideally, an owner and stakeholder should be agreed before the team leaves the room.

9. Finally, take time to review the session and offer every individual the chance to reflect with the group.

Maggie Grieve combines 30 years of global business-development leadership experience, team and executive coaching accreditations and her passion for facilitating lasting, positive change to help individuals and teams succeed and be happy in life and business.

Ideal Job Designer

Ingredients

Pen and paper

Optional: Post-it notes

Description

This tool helps clients identify their ideal job, or key satisfaction factors in their job, which can consequently be used for career planning and job search. The tool helps clients to focus on 'liked' and 'disliked' aspects of the current and previous jobs, so they get a complete understanding of what matters to them in the job and what makes the job most enjoyable for them. The tool helps clients to identify the common themes from their previous jobs, breaking these jobs down into satisfactory and unsatisfactory aspects. These aspects help them identify common factors. Sometimes, clients think a certain career would be ideal for them, but after analysing what brings them most satisfaction, they recognise that this 'ideal' job may not actually be the perfect fit they had assumed. The tool offers an organised approach to evaluating what the client wants and needs in their career/job. This newly gained clarity is often followed by new reflections and can lead to a more focused career change or job search plan.

Step by step

1. Use the table below and ask the client to list all the jobs held to date, including their current one.

Job	Liked	Disliked

2. Ask the client to reflect on what they liked and disliked in each of these jobs and make notes in the table in the appropriate columns. Spend as much time as needed on this step, asking sub-questions and encouraging the client to think deeper and identify as many likes and dislikes as they can. Ask them to be specific about each identified aspect, so the terms are not vague. If needed, ask them what specifically they mean under each term. Once the client has exhausted the list, ask them to take a step back, look at the list again, consider all previous jobs and check if anything relevant is still missing.
3. Ask the client to focus on the 'liked' column and reflect on any common themes. Ask them probing questions on whether they liked any particular job the most and why. Make notes on all the common themes.
4. Once common themes for the 'liked' column have been identified and exhausted, move to the 'disliked' column and ask the client to reflect on any common themes in this column, and to think of any previous jobs they particularly disliked and why. Make notes on all common themes.

Ideal Job
Designer

5. Ask the client to use a scale of 1–5 to evaluate the importance of each of the common themes identified under 'liked' (1 being not important and 5 being the most important).
6. Ask the client to do the same for the common themes identified under 'disliked' (1 being not-important and 5 being the most important).
7. Ask the client to share as many ideas as they can in regards to what jobs would have all the 'liked' common themes and as few as possible 'disliked' common themes. List these jobs in a new table, laid out as below:

Job	What I need/want	Rating	What the new job offers	Rating

8. Now, considering already identified 'liked' and 'disliked' themes, ask the client to think about what they would need/want in each of these jobs in order to match identified 'likes' and 'dislikes'. Encourage the client to frame these as positive rather than negative statements.
9. Ask the client to rate each of these on a scale of 1–10 (1 being the least and 10 the most important).
10. If the client has a specific job offer in mind, ask them to evaluate the new offer against the identified needs/wants and make notes in the table. Then ask them to rate each point on a scale of 1–10 (1 being the least and 10 the most important). Note: this final step can also be used for identifying the 'ideal' job and considering what needs/wants that job would satisfy and what their ratings would be. This can be a very helpful 'reality check' for the job they assume would be ideal for them.
11. If relevant, move into action planning for the new career/job search.

Reference

Jones, G., and Gorell, R. (2018) *50 Top Tools for Coaching: A Complete Toolkit for Developing and Empowering People* (4th edition). London: Kogan Page.

Jelena Jovanovic Moon is a Henley-trained coach and psychologist with degrees in coaching and organisational change and senior leadership roles in people management and organisational development.

Discovering Your 'IKIGAI'

Ingredients

Pen and paper

When does it work best?

The technique is particularly suitable for clients in transition and who are finding it difficult to know what they should/want to do next. This may include students at the start of their career, people in mid-career, thinking about making a change in direction, and those planning retirement. The technique works best when it is run over a number of coaching sessions, allowing adequate time for discussion and reflection.

Description

The IKIGAI tool is a set of questions that allow clients to explore and then unlock their unique purpose in life. It is based on looking at themselves through three different lenses, and then identifying where the overlap is between the three:

1. 'You Love It' – what energises you
2. 'You're Good at It' – you have the skills to make a difference
3. 'Reality Check' – it meets your practical requirements for (for example) salary, location and security, and you have (or can acquire) the necessary skills and qualifications.

In Japan, millions of people have *ikigai* – a reason to jump out of bed each morning. It has its origins on the island of Okinawa, which is said to be home to the largest population of centenarians in the world. It is one of the five zones identified in *The Blue Zones* (Buettner, 2012).

Step by step

1. The coach identifies suitable 'You Love It' questions, and then gets their client to answer them/talk them through and then write down their top 3–5 insights. Typical questions would focus on:
   o What energises you/drains your energy away
   o What you enjoyed doing as a child
   o What would be possible were money not a constraint
   o Jobs you'd love to do
   o Your priorities and values.
2. The coach identifies suitable 'You're Good at It' questions, and then gets their client to answer them/talk them through and then write down their top 3–5 insights. Typical questions would focus on:
   o Strengths, talents that come naturally
   o Jobs that others, who know you well, can see you doing
   o Considering your characteristics such as people skills, intellectual strengths, creativity, persistence and practical skills.
3. The client then drafts their 'IKIGAI' (one or two ideal new roles/careers to test in step 4).
4. The coach identifies suitable 'Reality Check' questions, and then gets their client to answer them/talk them through (using the 1–2 roles/careers identified in step 3) and then write down their top 3–5 insights. Typical questions include:
   o How well does it play to your passions and strengths as identified in steps 1 and 2?
   o How well does it meet your requirements? (Financial, location, work–life balance, work with 'purpose' etc.)

Discovering Your 'IKIGAI'

o Have you the skills (see step 2) and qualifications? If not, could you acquire them?

o Will this career still exist in 5–10 years?

o What's been holding you back so far?

5. Get the client to unlock their IKIGAI (the 'sweet spot' where all three sections overlap) – write it down! It could be more than one option, but don't let your client have too many options as this can lead to their subsequent efforts being diluted and unfocussed.

6. Get your client to translate this into an 'IKIGAI into Action' plan for the next 12–18 months.

o Identify priority themes and then supporting specific actions

o Agree how your client will monitor progress – is there an ongoing role for you as their coach?

While you can create your own questions, there are tailor-made resources available at the IKIGAI® Coaching Institute.

Reference

Buettner, D. (2012) *The Blue Zones: 9 Lessons for Living Longer from the People Who've Lived the Longest* (2nd edition). Washington: National Geographic.

Neil Munz-Jones is a Henley-qualified coach and business consultant who partners with Paul Donkers, the Founder of the IKIGAI® Coaching Institute.

The Influence Model

Ingredients

Pen and paper

Description

The Influence Model was first introduced by McKinsey in 2003 (Lawson and Price, 2003). The model identifies four building blocks for transformational change, which are informed by four prerequisites: fostering understanding and conviction; reinforcing changes through formal mechanisms; developing talent and skills; and role modelling. Often, in practice, disproportionate attention is paid to certain aspects of change, usually focusing on formal mechanisms.

Whilst the Influence Model can be used as a traditional management or consulting tool, it can also provide a very helpful framework for coaching conversations in the context of leadership of change, providing prompts for reflection, the development of self-awareness, identification of behaviour changes, and action planning.

When does it work best?

The Influence Model works well when leaders are about to embark on a major programme of change and want to explore how they can lead the change. It is also helpful in situations when leaders or others involved in change are frustrated by a lack of progress or by tensions and challenges. It can provide a diagnostic, reflective or action-planning tool.

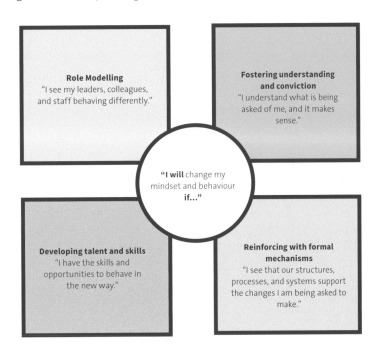

Step by step

1. Ask the client whether they would be interested in looking at a relevant model that might provide a helpful framework for discussion.
2. Draw out or list the core components of the model and briefly describe them, explaining that all of these need to be adequately considered for effective change to take place, yet that typically, in practice, they are not:
   a. Fostering understanding and commitment

The Influence Model

     b. Reinforcing with formal mechanisms

     c. Developing talent and skills

     d. Role modelling.

3. Ask the client for their initial reactions and reflections.
4. This may then naturally lead to a coaching conversation with respect to where attention is currently focused and where it needs to be focused, together with what leadership behaviours can support the change.
5. Useful prompts could include:

When planning a change

- Where have you focused your attention so far in your planning?
- How can you pay more attention to other components of the Influence Model?
- What does this mean for your leadership actions and behaviours?
- What does this mean for the change programme as a whole?
- How will you know you've been successful?

When currently involved in change (either as leader or participant in change)

- Which components are currently strong within the change programme?
- Which are weaker or have received less attention?
- Where do you think attention needs to be focused and how?
- What does this mean for your own actions and behaviours?
- What does it mean for others?
- How will you know that this is making a difference?

Reference

Lawson, E., and Price, C. (2003) The Psychology of Change Management. *The McKinsey Quarterly*, June.

Julie Flower is a leadership and team development coach, consultant and facilitator, specialising in navigating uncertainty in complex systems and applied improvisation.

Is it True?

Ingredients

Pen and paper

Set of questions

A4 page set out with three rectangular boxes labelled 'Evidence', 'Interpretation' and 'Impact'

When does it work best?

This tool is for clients who are stuck in the emotion of a situation. They may be prone to catastrophising, or to exaggerating or over-generalising the situation (e.g. "It always happens to me," "I never get positive feedback" or "They always do this"). Or they may struggle with confidence or Imposter Syndrome. It is a great tool for acknowledging where they are and allowing them the chance to move to a more resourceful space.

Description

This is a questioning and mapping tool used to help clients identify how much of the dilemma under discussion is based on genuine evidence (i.e. "is it true?"). It encourages them to consider whether some or all of it is their own extrapolation (or in other words, their fantasy or imagination expanding on the situation). It is based on the idea of evidence mapping with additional elements that add emotional impact and thinking. An element is also added from Byron Katie's questioning structure to identify truth (Katie and Mitchell, 2017).

Human nature causes us to seek recognition of our contribution, 'love' and security from others both at work and home. However, our limiting beliefs, lack of confidence or Imposter Syndrome can get in the way of our interpretation of what is happening around us. We sometimes seem to want to believe the worst. This exercise gently enables the client to refocus on the evidence and allows them to take a more objective view of what has been happening.

There are two stages to the process. The first enables a discussion about the scenario, what the client perceived was happening and how it impacted on them. The second stage is where you map the actual evidence that they have and how this reality might impact differently.

Step by step

Stage one:
1. Ask the client to talk about the scenario and what they believe they are experiencing.
2. Ask them how they are feeling in the scenario.
3. Ask them "Is that interpretation true?" Or "How true is your interpretation?"
4. If they answer "yes" to 3, ask "Do you absolutely know your interpretation is true?" (You are testing reality vs. perception/catastrophising here.)

Stage two:
5. Now you are mapping the following in the boxes on your page. Capture notes in the relevant boxes. You are exploring three areas:
   a. Evidence box – what actually happened? Here you are looking for facts. You are testing what would be observed if you or they were a fly on the wall in the situation. You are looking for things that you would both agree actually happened. What is the evidence? What did the other people say? How many times has it happened? What was the email? What do they know about the budget? The team? The scope? What has been said by the boss? The customer? The team members? What feedback has been given? What was the actual response to the

meeting? The presentation? The video? What was actually said, heard, experienced, felt?

    b. Interpretation box – how might they interpret this evidence differently? (Rather than how they appear to have interpreted it in stage 1.) As they look at what you have written, how would they interpret this objectively? What score would they give it out of 10? How would they rate their performance on the task? What words could they use to describe their work? What would you say as the fly on the wall?

    c. Impact box – as they look at the evidence and interpretation, what is their new choice about how they feel? Repeat this until all the feelings are captured.

6. Ask the client for their reflections about what you have done. What could they learn from this? How might they use this idea to help themselves in the future?

7. There might need to be some actions here – do they need to feedback any reflections to their team or their boss? What might they need to check for reality with their team/boss/customer? What might they be responsible for asking about or setting up to prevent any misinterpretation occurring again?

A great example of the use of this tool would be with a client who has doubts about how their boss or their team view the quality of their work/contribution.

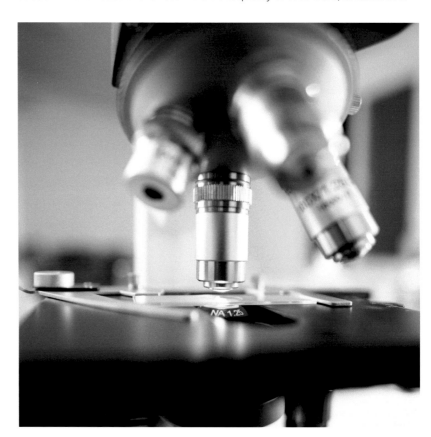

Reference

Katie, B., and Mitchell, S. (2017) *A Mind at Home with Itself*. London: Random House.

Fiona Moore is an experienced leadership coach, passionate about enabling others to be their healthy best. She runs her own business.

Metaphor Cards in Supervision

Ingredients

A deck of visual image cards

When does it work best?

This tool works well in a broad range of circumstances, particularly where the supervisee feels stuck or feels they are overanalysing the issue cognitively.

Description

The supervisee selects a card or cards to represent their enquiry, or aspects of their enquiry. The supervisor works with the supervisee to explore what the images might mean, how they might open new perspectives on the enquiry and new ways of moving forward. The tool also works well in group supervision, with the supervisees outlining their enquiry, and then the group members selecting cards that best represent the central issue to them.

Step by step

1. Ask the supervisee to provide some background to the supervision issue and then help them formulate a specific enquiry for the session.
2. If this feels like an appropriate approach for the enquiry, suggest and explain the approach to the supervisee, in particular how they will be using different parts of the brain to generate new insights.
3. Assuming they wish to proceed, introduce the supervisee to the cards – let them handle them and flick through the deck.
4. Ask them to pick the card that they think best represents their enquiry. Put the rest of the deck away.
5. With the card in front of the supervisee, begin to explore the image together.
6. Ask questions to help the supervisee generate new insights. For example:
   a. Where is the client in this image? Where are you?
   b. What stands out in the image? What might be hidden?
   c. What might be outside the card edges?
   d. What is happening in the card? What might happen next?
7. After the supervisee has fully explored the issue, help them integrate their insights. For example:
   a. What have you learned from the image?
   b. What do you know now that you didn't know at the start of the session?
   c. What now?
8. Ask the supervisee to put their card back in the deck.
9. Have a nice cup of tea and reflect on the session!

Mark Smith is an executive coach and supervisor who completed his MBA, MSc in behavioural change and Professional Certificate in Coaching Supervision at Henley Business School.

Mind Mapping

Ingredients

Paper

Pen

Description

Mind maps are frequently used in business and educational settings but they're also a great way to work with a coaching client. They create a diagram of thinking that can be explored together but where order isn't prioritised. Mind mapping encourages whole-brain thinking by bringing together logical, numerical and creative cortical skills to engage the brain in creative solution development.

When does it work best?

This tool is helpful for allowing a client to visualise concepts, problems and solutions. By drawing the situation out, coach and client can jointly look at what options might be available and what sticking points might exist. It's this approach that helps to encourage free-flow thought, whilst the map itself helps to demonstrate any links between topics that may have lain hidden up to that point. A client benefits from the coach asking different questions and providing different thoughts than they might ask or have thought of themselves. For agile coaching, the coach could take more of a mentoring role to provide valuable feedback to the client.

Step by step

1. Begin with the main concept/goal – what is the purpose of the conversation? Ask the client either to note their goal or to draw a picture/image of their goal in the middle of the sheet of paper. Ask them to take some time to personalise this with some colours or images that fit with their topic. This draws attention and triggers associations, as our brains generally respond better to visual stimuli.

2. Then ask the client to add branches to this main concept. The main branches that flow from the central image are the key themes. You can explore each of the themes in greater depth by adding child branches.

3. As they add branches to their map, suggest they keep their key-area descriptions as brief as possible by using keywords. This will allow a greater number of associations, compared to longer, more complex phrases. For example, "find a new career where I can use my skills" could be split into "career" and "use of skills". More possibilities for each branch can be explored with further sub/child branches (e.g. "skills" can be split into "existing", "new" and "old").

4. Steps 1–3 are a good foundation, but you can further enhance the thinking process by suggesting to your client that they add in further visual elements to the branches. This will act as a visual stimulus to recall more information. You can also suggest to your client that they colour code the map – using colours to categorise or highlight information to be able to more easily identify connections that they would not otherwise have discovered.

Maggie Grieve combines 30 years of global business-development leadership experience, team and executive coaching accreditations and her passion for facilitating lasting, positive change to help individuals and teams succeed and be happy in life and business.

Mind Mapping

The Magic of the Senses

Ingredients

Outdoor version:
Paper (A3 works well)

Coloured pens,
charcoals or pastels

Indoor version:
Musical instrument

Paper, pens,
charcoals or pastels

When does it work best?

It works best when clients: lack confidence; are experiencing stress; lack energy; are not accepting the positives about themselves; are suffering from Imposter Syndrome; or want to improve innovation skills. It helps with resilience, calm, wellbeing and stress-management. It is good practice for staying present and releasing worry about the past or future.

Description

This experience is all about being present, where clients draw what they hear, feeling the flow and excitement in that moment of creating something where there is no right or wrong. There are many benefits of using this approach, such as reducing stress and understanding more about how other people experience the same environment in different ways. It increases the ability to be present and still, taking in our surroundings with no judgements. The tool works very well in team and group coaching.

Step by step

Outdoor version

If the weather is dry, I prefer this version.

1. Find out where your individual client or group is now on their creativity, confidence, wellbeing and whatever else is coming up in the coaching conversation.
2. Introduce this tool, making links to that content and reassure the client/s that whatever comes will come, and that there is no right or wrong answer.
3. Hand out the drawing materials and ask the client/s to draw what they hear.
4. Go outside. Ask your person or group to find a spot where they feel comfortable and start drawing.
5. If clients start asking for more instructions, confirm that there are no more instructions and that they can interpret "draw what you hear" in any way they choose.
6. I recommend at least 30 minutes for the drawing. You can offer up to two hours depending on your session's structure. The longer time is especially effective for groups.
7. When the time is up, ask the client/s to come back together and talk through what they experienced and show their creations. This is great fun in groups where people have heard similar things and chosen to represent them in different ways.
8. Recommend that they keep the drawing as an anchor to the session, serving as a reminder of all the learning they have experienced.

If any clients are visually or hearing impaired, the outdoor version adapts well by concentrating on the sense that they can use. For example, if someone is hearing impaired, they should draw what they see or feel in any way they choose to. A sense of smell can also be used.

The Magic of the Senses

Indoor version

As above, but indoors with the music/sound of your choice. You may want to shorten the time spent on this indoors, given the environment. I have done this with students playing all sorts of music, which has been great fun, as the students comment and laugh about the music choices. And you can adapt to their choices too.

Harriet Pemberton is a leadership trainer, professional coach and writer, supporting clients to understand their own excellence, resilience and place in the world.

le flock of golden birds

ead so that she looked like

stem.

umble," she said quietly.

THE UNBREAKABLE V

Magic Wand

Ingredients

None required

When does it work best?

When a person is focused on thoughts about something or someone and this is the reason why they are stuck. These might be related to cultural expectations, or the client's percep-tions of external demands or expec-tations. The way the client thinks is the reason they cannot move forward.

Description

The Magic Wand technique is a powerful question used in Acceptance and Commitment Therapy that can help a client get clarity on their goals (Harris, 2009). It can also help a person see what is troubling them in a different way and helps them become unstuck. It does not work by getting the client to imagine a scenario where their problems have gone away, but rather gets the client to think about how they might act differently if they had a different relationship with their thoughts. Most clients will be familiar with the saying "If I had a magic wand I would…", so it is an easy image to conjure up in the mind of the client.

Step by step

1. Summarise the thoughts or barrier that the client has discussed with you that appears to be preventing the client from moving forward.
2. Ask the client to imagine that they have a magic wand.
3. Ask the client to describe how they might act differently if their magic wand meant that the issue identified in step 1 did not trouble them.
4. If you are doing values work, go on to ask the client how they might make goals that are more in line with their values, with their magic wand working as described.
5. Once the client has explored how they might act differently and what their goals might be, if their thoughts were not a problem, start to reflect on how unhelpful their current thoughts are. ACT uses mindfulness to help clients have different relationships with their thoughts. To notice when unhelpful thoughts arise but not to get entangled in these thoughts.
6. You might like to think about how you could make the magic wand reality a current reality and work with your client in the usual way to achieve this.

Reference

Harris, R. (2009) *ACT Made Simple: A Quick Start Guide to ACT Basics and Beyond*. Oakland, CA: New Harbinger Publications.

Claire Rason is a coach, the founder of profes-sional services consultancy Client Talk and host of the podcast *Lawyer's Coach*.

Magic Theatre

Ingredients

Attitude of mind: Suspend normal world criteria and rules

A sign: 'For mad people only. Price of admission: your mind' (optional)

Description

In the famous novel, *Steppenwolf*, by Hermann Hesse, the main character, Harry, feels trapped in his conventional life. One day he meets a magician who takes him to a 'Magic Theatre'. The sign on the door announces 'For madmen only. Price of admission: Your mind'. Inside the theatre are a multitude of doors, mirrors and passageways. Harry sees himself reflected; flat, thin, tall, short, upside down, rearranged. He comes to recognise that every human is a 'manifold world, a constellated heaven, a chaos of forms, of states and stages of inheritance and possibilities'. The magic theatre offers a world of possibilities where no idea is too bizarre. Every idea is tentative and subject to change. In this space, clients can play, avoid judgement and explore the opposite of their practical solutions of the real world.

When does it work best?

This technique works best when clients feel stuck or trapped by the assumptions, conventions and rules. The theatre provides an imaginative space for creative, free thinking to generate ideas without judgement.

Step by step

1. Describe the story of Harry in *Steppenwolf*.
2. Invite the client to close their eyes and imagine a walk through the Magic Theatre.
3. Allow the client to walk down several corridors and imagine different images of themselves.
4. With the client's eyes still closed, start to explore how the problem may look within the theatre mirrors: shorter, upside down or rearranged.
5. Invite the client to propose 2 or 3 solutions from within the imagined space, without evaluating them, using the real-world criteria.
6. Spend time dwelling in the magic of the solution in this space, as if the way of seeing the problem and the solution were real.
7. When returning to the real world, invite the client to consider what aspects of the 2 or 3 solutions could be employed.

Jonathan Passmore is a chartered psychologist, accredited coach, supervisor and director of the Henley Centre for Coaching, Henley Business School.

Magic Theatre

Noticing and Naming the Inner Critic

Ingredients

Attitude:
self-awareness

When does it work best?

The technique works best for clients who are experiencing low confidence and subsequent paralysis in decision-making and taking on new challenges. Often relevant for clients experiencing Imposter Syndrome (whereby their inner critic implies that they will be 'found out' for not being 'good enough'), it also complements other coaching approaches within a toolkit. For instance, it can be integrated into cognitive-behavioural techniques around distorted patterns of thinking and person-centred techniques of asking what is true and liberating.

Description

Mohr's (2015) interpretation of the 'inner critic' is a brilliantly relatable and constructive framework for helping a client to counter the inner voice of self-doubt that prevents them from making positive change. Mohr defines the inner critic as an inner voice of self-doubt that prevents an individual from moving forward. Examples of what the inner critic might say to an individual include "you are not sufficiently qualified/experienced/senior/skilled enough to take on a new challenge/project/opportunity". If the inner critic is loud enough or given enough mind-space, it can become the dominant way of thinking and cause paralysis in individual decision-making and change. There are several positive attributes to Mohr's framework. Firstly, it is gently supportive in encouraging individuals to recognise the inner critic. Secondly, it is non-confrontational in appreciating the positive motives of the inner critic for activating a safety blanket, while simultaneously questioning the helpfulness of the voice in achieving transformational goals. Finally, it is pragmatic in suggesting that the inner critic cannot be dispelled altogether but positive practices can instead be implemented to quieten it and amplify other more constructive influences.

Step by step

1. Notice the inner critic. Ask the client about the commonly voiced beliefs shared by the inner critic. For instance, ask "what does the inner critic say to you when you consider doing something that feels challenging/stretching/exciting?"
2. Create a character that personifies the inner critic. Ask the client, "if the inner critic were a real person, what would they be called/look like/sound like?"
3. Compassionately recognise and engage the motives of the inner critic. Ask the client "what do you think the inner critic is trying to protect you from?"
4. Encourage restating of the inner-critic voice by separating the 'I' from the voice in reflecting back. Ask the client to practise this, for instance: "my inner critic is saying that I am not good enough to undertake this challenge".
5. When the inner critic is heard, encourage the client to signpost it! Suggest a physical interruption, such as clapping or changing body position. Recommend a verbal response like "I've heard you – I thank you for trying to protect me but I've got this under control". Then encourage amplifying other more constructive influences.

Reference

Mohr, T. (2015) *Playing Big*. London: Arrow Books.

Pippa Ruxton is an international career and leadership coach providing rigorous, tailored and practical support, with extensive coaching experience and a successful corporate career.

Outcome Frame of Mind

Ingredients

Pen and paper

Post-it notes
(optional)

Description

This is a simple to use tool that helps clients get out of negative, problem-focused thinking. It helps them replace a 'problem' frame of mind with a more positive 'outcome' frame of mind. Clients sometimes tend to spend an extensive amount of time talking about the problem, describing it in detail and presenting it as an insurmountable issue. This tool breaks the mindset where client is absorbed with the problem and it is all they can talk about. The tool limits the time the client spends describing the problem and encourages them to take a different perspective on the situation. It gives them chance to take a step back, reconsider the context, adopt a bigger picture view and move into a solution-generating mode.

When does it work best?

It is helpful when a client feels stuck thinking and talking about the problem, rather than moving into a solution-focused mindset. It is beneficial for cases where the client is immersed in the 'problem'. This tool helps them reframe the situation, take a wider perspective and focus on desired outcomes, rather than the problem. It could be used for most problems.

Step by step

1. Explain to the client that you will be asking them two sets of questions, one set related to the problem and the other related to the outcome. Clarify with the client that they will have only a very limited time for the problem description stage (7–10 minutes).
2. Ask the client the following questions and make notes:
   - What is the problem?
   - How long has it been a problem?
   - What is the worst thing about this problem?
   - How often does the problem occur?
   - Who is to blame?
   - What has stopped you so far from solving this problem?
   - What are the major obstacles you face trying to solve the problem?
   - How does this problem make you feel, think, see, hear?

   Measure the time spent on this problem stage of the process and advise the client when the time has expired.
3. Move to the solutions and outcome stage of the problem. Ask the client the following questions and make notes:
   - What outcome do you want?
   - How will you know when you have achieved the outcome?
   - What possible solutions can you think of?
   - What resources do you need to achieve the outcome?
   - What resources do you have that will help you achieve the outcome?
   - How can you secure the additional resources you need?
   - When/where have you succeeded before in a similar situation?
4. Make notes on all possible outcomes, without filtering. (Possibly use Post-it notes to group them later.)

Outcome Frame of Mind

5. Once both sets of questions have been answered, encourage the client to reflect on the different perspectives, 'problem' and 'outcome'. Ask them to consider the differences in approach when focusing on problem vs. outcome. Ask for any learnings from it. If relevant, possibly share your perception on how their energy, tone and so forth changed from one stage to the other.
6. Move into action planning and help the client define next steps and timelines.

Reference

Jones, G., and Gorell, R. (2018) *50 Top Tools for Coaching: A Complete Toolkit for Developing and Empowering People* (4th edition). London: Kogan Page.

Jelena Jovanovic Moon is a Henley-trained coach and psychologist with degrees in coaching and organisational change and senior leadership roles in people management and organisational development.

Overcoming Change Inertia and Resistance in Team

Ingredients

Whiteboard or large piece of paper

Pens

Column 1 **Our Collective Goal (struggling to implement)**	Column 2 **Our Collective Inventory (doing or not doing instead)**	Column 3 **Our Collective Competing Commitments**	Column 4 **Collective Assumptions**
Create a culture of trust and unwavering support	We do not listen well to each other	We are each committed to not having to follow anyone else's direction and preserving our entrepreneurial spirit	We assume there is a conflict between entrepreneurship and collective collaboration
	We talk behind each other's backs	We are committed to winning even if it means others in the group will lose	That our present position will not last, that the lean times will come again – and when they do, there will be casualties
	We avoid difficult conversations	We are committed to overbooking ourselves to avoid being redundant	That there is more safety in hedging and overbooking
	We do not share information		

Example

Description

Change is vital to business progress but employee resistance to change can be a frustrating and costly challenge that ultimately results in increased employee turnover, decreased employee satisfaction and reduced productivity. Even when the benefits seem obvious, real deep and lasting adaptive change is fraught with excess challenge. Kegan and Lahey (2001) argue that it is the "immunity to change" that keeps us stuck. A common factor to this resistance is

Overcoming Change Inertia and Resistance in Team

the feelings the change invokes in people rather than the change itself and the reality of that change, and it's this that creates the impasse or resistance that can then become infectious across an organisation. Employee engagement in change can help to overcome this resistance. This tool enables leaders to engage employees and ensure their participation in understanding these 'social changes' in a practical and simple manner. This can help to avoid blind spots and can replace negative with positive attitudes towards the operational changes required.

When does it work best?

Using the technique enables the client to make their own efforts more effective at meetings where change is being discussed, because it helps teams to work together. With the coach, the teams collaborate, become more curious and start to question to understand the competing demands, assumptions and beliefs (often subconscious) that undermine the conscious assumptions and agreements they have made. This opening up to consider the change allows them to develop plans that will facilitate the change most effectively based on these new understandings. It's the framework for the tool that allows for resistance to be lowered, because it helps to shift attention away from the facts of plans, technical and operational details, work tasks and the anxiety these might create, towards what the changes will mean for stakeholders – staff, clients, suppliers and so on – and how they can work collaboratively to make this work better for everybody.

Step by step

1. Create a large grid with four columns and several rows on the whiteboard.
2. Collective Commitment Goals (column 1)
   Invite the team to identify the improvement goal(s) or changes they are committed to. You can suggest they review their team charter, objectives and working agreements for this. For existing commitments, ask them which they have been successful in implementing and which they have struggled to make happen. For new ones, ask them to articulate and agree them. Ideally, any new goals ought to be something that they want to achieve and have a high level of passion about and which others would affirm as worthy of their work and commitment. From this initial brainstormed list, ask them to identify the ones they are struggling to implement most and list these in the first of four columns. These are the collective commitment goals.
3. Collective Inventory (Column 2)
   Ask the team, either as a whole or in small subgroups, to record fearlessly, honestly and objectively all the behaviours they do, and don't do, that undermine their Column 1 collective goals. Use Column 2 for this. At this stage, you may notice the team start to observe their self-protective and self-defeating behaviour, so allow enough time for the ideas to flow and the team to relax into the task.

Overcoming Change Inertia and Resistance in Team

4. Collective Competing Commitments (Column 3)
   Ask the team to reflect on what they recorded in Column 2 and to think about what competing commitments are driving the actions behind the behaviours they recorded there. These should be recorded in Column 3. Give them plenty of time to consider these thoroughly. Prompt them using questions, including the AWE question ("and what else?").

5. Collective Assumptions (Column 4)
   Now invite the team to identify and explore the assumptions, beliefs or fears that sit behind these competing commitments. For example: "We assumed that if we did X then Y would happen." Record these in Column 4. By now, the team should start to see that this is where the really big change must occur. This is referred to as 'adaptive change' and it is this that is the important concept related to reducing a team's immunity or resistance to change.

6. Test of Assumptions and Action Planning (optional Column 5)
   Finally, explore how to overcome these limiting beliefs or at least to experiment with discovering whether they still hold true. You could add a Column 5 to record any ideas created to test the validity of the assumptions, and the outcomes of those experiments. These can start small and safe or be more radical, but they should form the basis of an agreed action plan moving forward.

Reference

Kegan, R., and Lahey, L. (2001) The Real Reason People Won't Change. *Harvard Business Review*, November, 84–93.

Maggie Grieve combines 30 years of global business-development leadership experience, team and executive coaching accreditations and her passion for facilitating lasting, positive change to help individuals and teams succeed and be happy in life and business.

Performance – Pressure Curve

Ingredients

Printed copy of the diagram

Pens

Paper

Whiteboard or flipchart

Description

It can be challenging for people to manage the balance between performance and pressure. This is a simple visual diagram that can help demonstrate some of the pitfalls and also where a state of optimum wellbeing can sit. It provides a diagrammatic representation that people can reflect upon and use to gain an initial perspective of where they may be at now, if they were to plot themselves on this diagram. There have been multiple different adaptations to the original diagram from that developed by Yerkes and Dodson (1908).

When does it work best?

This diagram can be useful if clients want to explore where their wellbeing is sitting now, or if concerns are raised about juggling workloads. It provides a client with a simple view and perspective of this. It allows a client to explore where they may be heading on this curve if things remain unchanged, and if there are increases or decreases in either performance or pressure demands over a period of time.

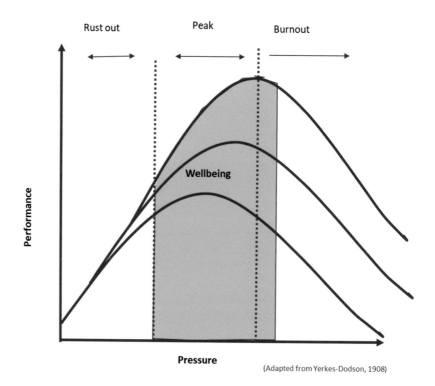

(Adapted from Yerkes-Dodson, 1908)

Step by step

1. Draw the diagram on paper, whiteboard or flipchart.
2. Provide a brief overview of what this diagram represents. For example, "This is a very simple representation of where a state of 'wellbeing' may sit, and shows that there are optimal levels of performance and pressure that support this. There is also a spectrum, by which if there is not enough or too much pressure, there may be a risk of burning out or rusting out."

Performance – Pressure Curve

3. Ask the client to then plot on the diagram where they are sitting now. If this is being used with a leader, then ask the client to plot where they and their team are sitting now.
4. There are multiple directions in which this can lead with a client, and here a few additional questions that may be useful: "If this is where you are now, could you plot where you would like to be?" "What would that look like, and feel like?" "What would you need to do differently?" and "What resources and support are available to you?"
5. If the client plots themselves in the 'wellbeing zone', it can be useful to ask the client questions like: "How will you sustain this?" and "What are any potential watch outs for you going forward?"

Reference

Yerkes, R.M., and Dodson, J.D. (1908) The Relation of Strength of Stimulus to Rapidity of Habit Formation. *Journal of Comparative Neurology of Psychology*, 18(5): 459–82.

Deb McEwen is an experienced accredited coach who has held senior leadership roles (NZ, AU and UK) and has an extensive background in health and wellbeing.

PAC (The Parent, Adult, Child of Transactional Analysis)

Ingredients

A diagram of the ego state model (PAC)

Paper and pen

Description

In 1964, Eric Berne created the theory of Transactional Analysis, based on the Id, Ego and Super Ego structural theory of Sigmund Freud (1923). Berne (1964) noted that during social interactions, from time to time people may show noticeable changes in their behaviour, which are often accompanied by emotional shifts, and that such shifts correspond to a particular state of mind. Together, such feelings, behaviours and thoughts created their own systems, known as ego states. Berne referred to Freud's Id as the Child ego state, the Ego as the Adult ego state, and the Super Ego as the Parent ego state. The parent state is the behaviours, thoughts and feelings copied from parents and parental figures; the child state is the behaviours, thoughts and feelings which are replayed from our childhoods; and the adult state is our behaviours, thoughts and feelings as direct, objective responses to the here and now. From being on the receiving end of our parents (or parental figures), they teach us the job of *nurturing* or *chastising*. We then learn how to repeat those behaviours onto others. As children, we experience our emotions or feelings of *adapting* to our parents' (or parental figures) teachings or *rebelling* against them; our desire to be free of the perceived restrictions of their authority.

When does it work best?

As a social psychology theory for personal change and growth, the PAC model can be applied in counselling, educational, organisational and psychotherapeutic specialisations, and indeed in any area where there is an identified need to understand communication and relationships between individuals (Stewart and Joines, 1987). It works best when considering why certain relationships are not yielding the desired outcome or when exploring the upsides and downsides of assumed roles within existing relationships.

An example of where PAC might be used is where a client is having difficulties managing a report, or vice versa. In such an instance, the coach may hear the client report that, *"I told my husband a million times: I keep telling you, but you never listen!"* (chastising parent) or *"I'm better off doing the spreadsheet myself. She'd just mess it up and I'd end up doing the work anyway – not that I'd tell her that, of course!"* (nurturing parent) or *"I'm happy just to go along with everyone else really"* (adapting child) or *"And I thought to myself, if he talks to me like that again (actor: chastising parent), I'll tell him where to stick his job"* (re-actor: rebelling child).

If behaving as the chastising or nurturing parent, or behaving as the adaptive or free child, will not provide a positive outcome to an interaction (I'm ok and you're ok), then the interlocutors need to choose an adult-to-adult conversation. If the active parties maintain a basic emotional intelligence by responding to the here and now in a rational, reasonable, logical and objective state, they will have a better chance of achieving their desired outcome.

PAC (The Parent, Adult, Child of Transactional Analysis)

Step by step

1. Ask the client to describe a current relationship that is not yielding the desired outcome.
2. Next, ask the client to write down a goal statement that encompasses the changes they would like to make to that relationship. It can be written in whatever way comes to mind, so long as it's framed positively. For example, rather than *"I want X to stop micromanaging me"*, this can be reframed as *"I want X to grant me more autonomy"*.
3. Explain the PAC model to the client and why you've identified from the issue that it may be relevant.
4. Ask the client to write 'Parent', 'Adult' and 'Child' in two columns next to each other (as above). Then ask the client to head the first column with their own name and the second with the name of the subject of the issue presented within the coaching session.
5. Explain each ego state (as described in 'Description' above).
6. Invite the client to draw an arrow between column one and column two to signify the dynamic of the described relationship.
7. Use Socratic questioning to explore why the client has chosen this dynamic and what evidence confirms to them the existence of this dynamic.
8. Ask the client to state the positives and negatives of this dynamic in helping both parties achieve their desired outcome.
9. Now ask the client which new relationship dynamic would better serve both parties' purposes, and deeply explore why; ask the client to list and write down the benefits.
10. Ask the client to write down a list of everything that needs to happen in order for this new relationship dynamic to exist. Use the phrase "What else?" to encourage the client's deeper thinking. Ask them also to consider this question from the perspective of the second person and from the perspective of the system in which they work (family, team, organisation, etc.).
11. Ask the client to remove from the above list (step 10) any actions that are unrealistic, unsafe or unreasonable.
12. Ask the client what these changes would mean for them and the other person – what would be the impact and consequences?
13. Ask the client, "If these changes happen, what will be the necessary sacrifices, for you and others, and are these sacrifices worth the change?"
14. Ask the client what commitments they will make to themselves to make the necessary changes in order to yield the outcome(s) they desire, and how they and others will know when these actions/goals have been achieved.

References

Berne, E. (1964) *Games People Play: The Psychology of Human Relationships*. Penguin books. Repr. New York: Grove Pr.

Freud, S. (1923) The Ego and the Id. *TACD Journal*, 17(1): 5–22. doi:10/gg6s36.

Rock, D. (2008) SCARF: A Brain-based Model for Collaborating with and Influencing Others. *NeuroLeadership Journal*, 1(1): 44–52.

Stewart, I., and Joines, V. (1987) *TA Today: A New Introduction to Transactional Analysis*. Nottingham; Chapel Hill: Lifespace Pub.

Callum O'Neill is a Henley coach specialising in executive, team and systems coaching, with a particular interest in double and triple loop learning.

Overcoming Conflict in Teams

Ingredients

Optional whiteboard/ flipchart and pens

When does it work best?

Conflict doesn't need to be a negative force. Bringing conflicts out into the open, where they can be resolved, is important and effective. The most productive and effective teams appear to be the ones where there is high diversity but where members have developed robust yet sensitive ways of managing conflict (Mosakowski and Earley, 2000). This technique allows a coach to help teams align around an area of conflict where this has already occurred and is causing friction. The exploration is done together in a spirit of 'fault-free conflict management'.

Description

Conflict – antagonistic interactions in which one party tries to block the ideas, actions or decisions of another party – is a common and destructive occurrence in teams. In general, the more diverse a team, the greater the potential for conflict. Fortunately, it is also the case that the greater the diversity, the higher the potential for creativity. Conflicts can arise as a result of a multitude of issues:

1. *Substantive/task* conflicts are based around goals, tasks and how things are done
2. *Emotional/relationship* conflicts arise from, for example, jealousy, insecurity, annoyance, personality clashes or misunderstandings
3. *Process* conflicts are centred around how duties and resources are allocated.

The following describes a way of coaching with a team using a four-step mechanism to resolve a conflict caused by an unresolved task or process conflict that has led to relationship conflict.

Step by step

1. **Topic**: work with the leader to understand more about their understanding of the conflict and identify which individuals or team members should be part of the exercise. Work with your client to invite these team members to a meeting.
2. **Briefing**: set out the approach and the rules to all participants.
3. **Reconfirm the position**: in this step, the coach works with the team to articulate areas of disagreement. Questions can include:
   - What do you violently agree on?
   - Are you prepared to accept that each of you is acting with goodwill?
   - Are we looking for broadly the same outcome?
   - What do you respect the other party for?

Reinforce with all attendees that no-one can be negative or accusatory.

4. **Fault-free task analysis**: continuing with the no-blame rule, encourage each team member individually to explain what they are trying to achieve and why? Explore what is preventing them from achieving this? ('Nancy Kline's Time to Think, Thinking Environment teachings including Timed Talk could be used here to ensure everyone is included in this exercise – see 'References'.) Again, it is critical to reinforce with participants that their reasons given cannot be to blame someone else. Follow this up with questions that explore a view of what the implications are for stakeholders and how the team's goals are being affected. Perhaps create a brainstorming board to capture these ideas.
5. **Fault-free emotional analysis**: the previous steps have ensured that discussion is as rational as possible. That can be difficult because so much of conflict is centred around emotion. So, finally, this is the point

when the team members are encouraged to talk about how they feel and how they would like to feel. Ask questions that engage curiosity and creativity about what would enable them to change how they felt. This allows the emotional component of the conflict to be aired but reduces or eliminates the desire to blame.

6. **Solution generation**: it is important at this stage to make sure participants do not regress into confrontation. To support this, ask each member of the team to offer in turn at least one action that they could take individually that would help someone from the other side of the conflict divide. These should be related to helping them achieve what they are trying to do and how they want to feel. Each participant should also be asked to name or outline one thing that the team could do collectively.

7. **Conclusion**: it is important to keep reminding participants about the rules and the contract entered into at the start of the meeting – the tendency will be to revert to more negative forms of conversation if left unchecked. However, continuing to practise this process, the team will find they can resolve specific conflicts as well as absorbing the process and behaviours to address future conflicts at an earlier stage.

References

Kline, N. (1999) *Time to Think*. London: Cassell.

Kline, N. (2015) *More Time to Think*. London: Cassell.

Mosakowski, E., and Earley, P.C. (2000) A Selective Review of Time Assumptions in Strategy Research. *Academy of Management Review*, 25, 796–812.

Maggie Grieve combines 30 years of global business-development leadership experience, team and executive coaching accreditations and her passion for facilitating lasting, positive change to help individuals and teams succeed and be happy in life and business.

Energy Renewal

Ingredients

Energy Management
Grid diagram

Description

This exercise draws on the work of Tony Schwartz. It looks at the client's energy as a resource that can be systematically expanded and regularly renewed by introducing specific habits and behaviours in the area of their physical, mental, emotional and spiritual wellbeing. Coach and client spend time looking at how these can become unconscious and automatic through intentional practice.

Step by step

1. Invite the client to review each of the four elements of personal energy using the quadrant grids of physical, social/emotional, mental and spiritual energy.
2. With the client, identify the activities that build their energy. For example, what physical activities do they engage in that make them feel energised? Who do they spend time with that helps them build back their energy level? What mental tasks, such as reading or a crossword, help them to restore their energy? And finally, what spiritual practices, such as prayers, meditation and attending church, help them to renew their energy?
3. With the client, identify the activities that drain their energy.
4. Explore with the client how they can spend time undertaking energy-building activities.
5. Explore how they can make these activities a regular practice.
6. Help the client to develop a plan to renew energy levels by engaging in activities that are energising. Help them to recognise that, like a battery, these energy levels decline without regular top-ups.

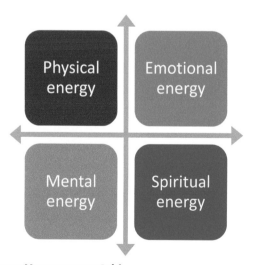

Diagram: Energy Management Grid

Jacqui Zanetti is an executive coach with a corporate background and a strong interest in international leadership.

Personal SWOT Analysis

Ingredients

A large piece of paper or whiteboard, pens, sticky notes

When does it work best?

A personal SWOT analysis works well when clients would like to consider their own personal development, raising their self-awareness and enabling them to better understand where they would like to focus their development in the future. It also works well for clients who are at a point of transition and considering a change of career. By being encouraged to critically evaluate themselves and their career, they may start to find new avenues to explore and gain a greater sense of their transferable strengths and skills, as well as start to work on what could get in the way or work against them.

Description

A SWOT analysis is a commonly used tool to help rapidly and critically evaluate factors relating to particular projects, organisations or strategies (Learnt, Christiansen, Andrews and Guth, 1969). However, carrying out a personal SWOT analysis can be a helpful tool for clients to take stock of their current situation and explore how they can move forward in their own development. By exploring strengths, weaknesses, opportunities and threats (or barriers), clients are encouraged to critically consider both internal and external factors in relation to their development.

SWOT encourages the generation and consideration of relevant factors, to encourage a balanced approach and avoid only focusing on the negative (or indeed only focusing on the positive). The process of identification of the issues can be helpful in itself and then lead to further exploratory coaching conversations to support clients to make the most of their strengths and opportunities, to positively address weaknesses and to seek to minimise threats or barriers. Whilst, within business, strengths and weaknesses are often internally focused and opportunities and threats, externally focused, this may be different with a personal SWOT. For instance, a future 'threat' to development and success may be related to a personal/internal factor, such as a client's lack of confidence in their own ability to learn a new skill.

Step by step

1. Ask the client to draw a large grid and label the sections 'strengths', 'weaknesses', 'opportunities' and 'threats/barriers'

STRENGTHS	WEAKNESSES
OPPORTUNITIES	THREATS

2. Ask them to consider each section in turn and write a different factor per sticky note, which they then place in the relevant section. As a coach, you may need to ask some prompting questions to encourage the client to identify as many relevant factors as possible, particularly if they tend to dwell on any one section of the grid. On further reflection, the client may move certain factors around the grid.

Personal SWOT Analysis

3. Once the SWOT analysis has been completed, spend time in each section of the grid asking questions to encourage the client to identify the most important or pressing factors. You can then work together to further explore these and develop tangible actions and motivation, whether to build on strengths, address weaknesses, make the most of opportunities or manage/minimise/prepare for threats.

4. One of the limitations of a traditional SWOT analysis is that it can generate a long list of relevant factors but then does not easily translate to a 'so what?' for action and next steps. That is where the coaching conversation can be so beneficial. The SWOT analysis provides the basis for exploration, challenge and identification of goals, over the course of one session or potentially throughout a coaching relationship. It can also be an iterative process. As new issues arise, they can be added to the SWOT analysis and considered in relation to the other factors.

5. It is useful to ask the client to keep a copy of the SWOT analysis to refer to in coaching sessions and as they work in between.

Reference

Learned, E.P., Christiansen, C.R., Andrews, K., and Guth, W.D. (1969) *Business Policy, Text and Cases*. London and Homewood, IL: Irwin.

Julie Flower is a leadership and team development coach, consultant and facilitator, specialising in navigating uncertainty in complex systems and applied improvisation.

Pick and Mix People

Ingredients

'Pick and Mix People' game (Orchard Toys)

Phone with a camera

Description

This well-loved children's card game is very easily adapted for coaching. You can have some fun creating images that represent where your client is right now in an area of their work or life, and from this identify outcomes for the coaching. The pictures on the cards require the client to think creatively about metaphors, which can be applied to day-to-day activity and skills or deeper discussions around identity and purpose. The cards enable your client to work with their own metaphor and to think creatively about what might represent their current situation. It is a great starter activity to uncover a development need or outcome for a coaching conversation, plus an inspiring way to close a session as you focus on the client's inner strengths to move forward and take action. It works just as well for exploring a stuck state as well as to develop an aspiration or goal. I've applied it to a multitude of coaching topics and it works well as a team activity too.

When does it work best?

This activity works best when it is applied to a role (current or aspirational) that your client would like to explore, such as being a successful leader, manager, coach, learner, a job role or something else. It works well face to face or remotely in 10–15 minutes as a quick starter activity or, if you prefer, you can explore what emerges in some depth over a longer conversation. For face-to-face use, spread out the cards on the table. If you want to use it for remote coaching, you'll need to make sure the client has a box of cards in advance. The beauty of this tool is that you can be playful and bring in some humour.

Step by step

1. Establish the role or situation your client would like to explore.
2. Lay out all the cards randomly and face up on the table. The client choses the feet, body and head that represents them in this situation in the present time.
3. Avoid giving directions or an explanation of how to make the choices – allow the client to make an instinctive choice based on their personal criteria. This will generate the metaphor for their current situation that has the most meaning. Take a photo.
4. Ask your client to explain their choice and ask what each of the cards represents in their current situation. This is likely to uncover their current behaviours, capabilities, skills, feelings, beliefs, values and purpose. Explore the detail of their metaphor and what it represents for them in their situation. You could focus on strengths or opportunities for growth or both. Find out how they are feeling, what they are thinking, being, hearing and seeing that is represented by their choice of cards. (If time is short, go straight to step 7.)

*Pick and Mix
People*

5. Here are some examples of questions that I like to use at this stage:
   - What are your thoughts and what are you thinking?
   - Are you achieving the relationships you need and want in this role?
   - Are you achieving the results/performance you need and want in this role?
   - And what do you want to have happen?
6. At this point, you can continue the coaching by exploring the avenues that emerge as appropriate and according to time available. The coaching would then flow naturally into step 7.
7. Lay out all the cards randomly and face up on the table again. Ask the client to choose the feet, body and head that represents them at their best. They can keep any of the current cards or change them. An alternative is to ask them to pick the cards that represent them being effective in the future situation/role or achieving the role they want. Take a photo and explore their choice of cards/metaphor. A gap analysis could be a good framework for discussion if you have time.
8. Ask the client to identify a place to display the photo of the cards that represent them at their best – perhaps as a screensaver, or printed out and pinned on a message board or inside their notebook or journal.

Variations

Step 2 – Variation 1 – Lay the cards out face down in three separate piles (one pile each for feet, body and head). This takes a bit more organising in advance, but increases the level of creativity required from the client. Chose a random card from each pile and turn it over to create a random person. Ask the client to create connections between each card and the personal learning/ideas that it represents

Step 2 – Variation 2 – Which cards would another person choose? It can be enlightening to step into the shoes of their manager, team colleague or business partner (etc.) and imagine their choice of cards. This could the be compared to their self-perception. They could even take the cards away and ask the other person to do this for real, as a creative way to generate genuine feedback.

Step 7 – Variation 3 – The Client chooses the feet, body and head that represents who they would like to be in that role or in the role to which they aspire. This works especially well for discussions around leadership development or for setting up a new business.

Clare Smale is an experienced and accredited coach and supervisor, and has published two coaching books as well as running her own business, inspired2learn.

The Pie of Time

Ingredients

Paper and pen

When does it work best?

It works best when a client is overwhelmed by tasks at work and recognises that they are not spending time on what they see as the right things, but have been unable find a way forward.

Description

This tool simplifies complexity. It is designed to draw out the current melee of activities at work that the client is unhappy or stressed about, and to define the future desired activities, highlighting the areas that are priorities. It is a simple, effective tool to discover where the client is now, in relation to tasks at work, and where they want to be, with an action plan to make this a reality. It builds on 'The Wheel of Life' tool, focusing specifically on activities at work. For example, what is the client spending time on that is not within their true scope of work? Are there opportunities for delegation or transference to other areas? Is the client able to tackle smaller/quicker tasks during specified times more efficiently? The process often uncovers time-management issues or tasks that should be being done by other members of staff, perhaps more junior, where the senior client has been promoted away from day-to-day processing, but still gets involved. By using the tool, the outcome often releases time to prioritise important working relationships and other priorities, often helping the client to identify their overall working-life goals.

Step by step

1. Introduce the idea of 'The Pie of Time' and explain that we will draw out how much time is spent on current work activities in a pie shape, and create a new pie for the future. I sometimes lighten the experience by asking the client about their favourite pies and they enjoy the chance to talk about food!
2. Start with the first pie and ask the client to list out all the activities they do now.
3. If they start talking about what they really should be doing, bring them back to what they do **now**.
4. Help them to think about the percentage of time spent on each activity.
5. Ask your client to draw a circle on their paper so that they can draw in the activities and the percentage of time spent in each section.
6. Often, the activities add up to more than 100%, and clients may draw a box outside the circle to represent this overspill.
7. The light begins to dawn on the client at this point about their priorities for the role, and how they want to spend time on things outside of work too.
8. Ask them to choose a time in the future by when they want to have made the changes. Six months works well.
9. Ask the client to draw another circle (their second pie) representing the desired situation in, for example, six months' time, talking through the real priority tasks. Coach them through who else can help with the remaining tasks.

The Pie of Time

10. I often find that the client has taken on things outside their scope because they are helpful and expert in their area. They typically know who the tasks should be reallocated to.
11. Continue the conversation, asking the client about the future tasks and if they are now content with the six-month pie picture. Does this fit with the role as it should be? Is there anything else? At this point, the client is often energised and can visualise their new ways of working on the right things.
12. Using this energy, continue to ask questions around what they can do, now and each month, to achieve this new Pie of Time and how they will hold themselves accountable, creating a clear action plan. Who else can help?
13. At this point, you should find the client becoming confident, very happy with the clarity and looking forward to making the changes to reach their ideal work-scope.

Harriet Pemberton is a trainer, professional coach and writer. She empowers clients to bring about changes they desire and to discover their excellence and life purpose.

Plasticine™ (Modelling Clay)

Ingredients

Plasticine™
(various colours)

Sheet of paper

When does it work best?

This is particularly useful during a coaching engagement when the coach would like to create more insight into a specific situation, goal or problem when a client seems to be stuck (van Nieuwerburgh, 2014). In GROW terms, it is most useful at the Reality stage.

Reference

van Nieuwerburgh, C. (2014) *An Introduction to Coaching Skills, A Practical Guide*. London: Sage.

Maggie Grieve combines 30 years of global business-development leadership experience, team and executive coaching accreditations and her passion for facilitating lasting, positive change to help individuals and teams succeed and be happy in life and business

Description

The client is given some modelling clay to mould, to help draw out conversation and insight on the topic being discussed. The focus is on encouraging the client to use their hands as they talk, shaping, moulding and playing with the object. For many clients, this physicality appears to enable a deeper conversation, leading to fresh insights that may not have emerged had the coach and client just engaged in a traditional conversation.

Step by step

1. Give the client a lump of Plasticine™ or modelling clay and ask them to shape it in any way that represents their current situation. Be careful to provide no further real instruction at this point but do be clear that it does not need to look like any specific thing and that a shape is fine.
2. Once the client has moulded the clay into a shape they are happy with, ask them to describe how this relates to their own situation.
3. Continue the coaching session in the normal way, using the object created as a discussion anchor. Place the piece of Plasticine™ on a sheet of paper in view of you and your client during the session so it can easily be referred to.

Quick Coherence

Ingredients

Bio feedback device measuring heart-rate variability (optional)

Mobile/laptop/tablet (optional)

Description

The quick coherence technique is part of HeartMath, a system of simple and powerful self-regulation techniques that are easy to learn and designed to be used 'in the moment', whatever the situation. The technique brings the premise of adding heart to a client's interactions and all that they do, meaning that they can bring their best self to their professional, social and personal lives. Bringing coherence is not relaxation; it is a separate 'doing' state within the autonomic nervous system – a doing state that enables flexibility and adaptability to demands and is therefore potentially more appropriate for many daily activities. The state of coherence is both psychologically and physiologically distinct from the state achieved through most relaxation techniques.

When does it work best?

The quick coherence technique works best in the moment, when dealing with a situation of stress and pressure. It can be used on a daily basis to build a base level of resilience within people. The client is shown the technique and encouraged to use it daily for short periods of time, somewhere between two and five minutes to begin with. This is linked with talking through the impact and effect of emotions on the client's performance and effectiveness. Both of these build awareness in the client of their intention versus impact, and build self-regulation capabilities.

Step by step

1. Work with your client to build their understanding of how stress and overwhelm impact them physically and psychologically. Introducing the quick coherence technique from HeartMath provides a tool for your client to use to prep themselves for a potentially stressful meeting or situation, and something for them to use in the moment to assist in self-regulation. Creating a state of coherence can be done in 60 seconds, and releases stress and stops draining emotions.
2. Firstly, focus on the area around your heart, moving your consciousness from your pre-frontal cortex to your heart. Heart Focus.
3. Secondly, think about and imagine breathing through your heart. Breathing in and out for longer and more deeply than you would usually do. Heart Breathing.
4. Thirdly, deliberately engage a positive emotion, something that makes you feel connected, happy, joyful, content and positive. Heart Appreciation.

Sarah Perrott is a Henley- and HeartMath-accredited executive coach specialising in working with clients to build mental fitness, resilience and wellbeing.

The Rocking Chair

Ingredients

Optional: a room with sufficient space and an extra chair

Description

This tool can be used as a variation on the time machine tool. It is mainly useful when the goal is a lifetime ambition. For example, a client might say they have always aspired to be a chief executive and they want to dedicate their coaching sessions towards that goal. The coach should establish the importance of the goal with the client before proceeding, to avoid focusing on a 'nice to have' objective. The tool offers the client an opportunity to visualise where they would like to be in the future, to assess the scale of the challenge ahead and to start to define their success metrics, were they to achieve that success.

Step by step

1. Ask the client what their favourite place in the world is; perhaps somewhere where they are just happy to sit still and enjoy the experience.
2. If there is space to manoeuvre in the room, ask the client to move to a different chair and imagine themselves sitting in a rocking chair in the favourite place they have identified. If there is no extra chair in the room, you could also ask the client to turn their chair slightly to make them realise they are stepping into a different perception universe. The physical movement into a different position is often helpful when asking coachees to step into a different dimension.
3. You can also help transport them there by asking them to paint a picture for you of what they feel and see.
4. Ask the client to visualise themselves on a rocking chair and sitting in this favourite place surrounded by loved ones (or a journalist or documentary film crew) who are keen to hear their story.
5. It may be worth using the analogy of Rose, in the movie *Titanic*, to ask the client to look back at the moment they realised they had achieved their lifelong ambition and describe it to you:
   "Imagine you are in your twilight years and you have achieved [insert their goal, making use of their own words as much as possible]. *You are sitting on a rocking chair and telling your story?"*
6. Invite the client to describe to you what success looked like for them: *"What was the first thing you noticed that told you that you had been successful? What else?"* Explore the circumstances.
7. Invite the client to move back to their normal chair, in the present. Give them a moment to recover and reflect, then ask them whether they have learnt anything from the exercise that they did not know before.
8. Given where we are now in this session: *"What would be useful for us to focus on?"* Ensure that the client is as specific as possible on clarifying the goal.
9. What outcome are they looking for from the session?
   - *"What would need to happen in our session today that would make this conversation worthwhile for you?"*

The Rocking Chair

- *"At the end of our session together today, what do you want to have achieved?"*
- *"What would make today's session a success for you?"*

10. Help the client explore their current reality. Examples of exploratory questions include:
    - *"Why is it important to start to address this now?"*
    - *"What is happening at the moment that gives you confidence you can achieve this goal? Anything else?"*
    - *"On a scale of 1 to 10, 1 being the beginning of your journey towards this goal and 10 being its achievement, where are you now?"*

11. Partner with the client to help them start to develop a plan of action.
    - *"Given what we have discussed (some of the ideas that have been suggested to you), are there any options you have mentioned that you would like to try?"*

12. Wrap-up the session by getting the client to confirm what actions they are committing to and building in an accountability process (e.g. committing to a timescale). Also help them to think about what could hinder their progress.

13. Partner with the client to end the session.

Taff Gidi is partner and executive coach at hi5 Coaching and a chartered governance professional with experience as a principal adviser to boards.

Sailboat Retrospective

Ingredients

Whiteboard or flipchart

Pens

Post-it notes (two colours)

Description

The Sailboat technique helps to define a vision and identify what will help to achieve that vision. It is normally used to facilitate team discussion by providing a platform for reflection. It is essentially built around the GROW model and can be adapted easily for equally effective use with individuals or small businesses, and used in person or online using a shared whiteboard facility. The Sailboat helps define a purpose, identify resources, risks and obstacles as well as potential routes for change and a forward-moving action plan, in a fun, tactile and visual way.

When does it work best?

The Sailboat tool works well with both large and small teams who would benefit from reflecting on the whole GROW model together – to gain a picture of their goals, their current reality, their options and the identification of what actions they will take together to create maximum value for themselves as individuals and as a high-functioning team. The tool description provided here highlights the process when used in a team setting, but can easily be adapted for use in one-to-one coaching, where it is equally effective.

Step by step

1. **Draw a boat and an island**
   Invite the members of the group to draw a boat. The style is up to them (pirate boat, cruise ship, container ship, etc.) but it must have a body, sails and an anchor. Draw an island – they can add extras to the setting, such as sunshine, clouds, stormy seas and so forth.

2. **Name the boat**
   Agree the topic of discussion and invite the team to name the boat.

3. **Agree the mission (goal)**
   Ensure every member of the group has Post-it notes in the first colour and a pen. Invite the team to think about what their boat represents, the topic or theme (e.g. a project, an event, a problem, the team). Invite them to write their mission on their Post-it notes – where do they want to set sail to, what do they want to achieve (i.e. what is their goal)? Add these to the hull of the boat. Discuss any differences to create a consensus.

Sailboat Retrospective

4. **Add sails and anchors (reality)**
   Invite the team to now add 'sails' and 'anchors', using the same colour of Post-it note as they used for the mission.
   - *Sails* – these represent what's good and going well
   - *Anchors* – these represent the things limiting their progress.
   Ask them to review all the sails and anchors and group them as appropriate. If something is a sail *and* an anchor, suggest this is clarified on the note. Again, duplicates are welcome as they may include subtle differences to be explored and they demonstrate shared views, thus producing a bigger sail or anchor.

5. **Scale the sails and anchors (reality)**
   Invite the teams to scale each one of their sales and anchors between -10 and +10. Teams should discuss each note, seek to agree its meaning and then decide as a group where on the scale it should be. If it helps, the teams can vote by writing on it rather than having to agree verbally. This allows individual views to be more freely expressed and discussed.
   The rating should equate to how powerful these items are in either allowing their boat to sail or in holding it back. For example, +2 would be a relatively small sail and +9 would be a mainsail. Alternatively, a -7 anchor may be almost stopping them moving forward whereas a –1 anchor isn't really restricting momentum significantly.
   This process is really effective at encouraging group discussion as well as raising awareness of issues and opportunities across the team and their impact on the team. Additional sticky notes can be used again here, if helpful.

6. **Raising the sails and anchors (options)**
   Once all sails and anchors have been discussed and scored, give each member of the team the second-colour Post-it notes. Encourage their imagination at this point and ask them to think of suggestions or actions that would raise one of the sails or anchors on the boat. Encourage thinking of small or incremental ideas that would help by even just one point.
   Invite them to capture these ideas on the new-colour Post-it notes for placing beside the relevant sail or anchor. If they can't be placed beside a sail or anchor, they can be placed somewhere else on the map as ideas for making the ship go faster.
   Questions to prompt debate include:
   - What else? (You can keep asking "and what else?"!)
   - Is this bigger or smaller than the last item we scaled?
   - If you could cut away one anchor, which would it be? How could you do that?
   - If you could raise one sail to +10, which would it be? How could you do that?
   - What would happen if all anchors were cut away? What would change?
   - If you could add an 'iron sail' (an engine!) to your boat, what would it be?
   - How can we raise this sail from a +5 to a +6?
   - How can we raise this anchor from a -7 to a -6?

Sailboat Retrospective

If there are numerous suggestions for raising sails and anchors, work with the team to discuss and rank these individually and then agree which improvements to take forward and in what order by discussing the logistics of the improvement (e.g. who could own or be engaged in the task? how big is it? how long will it take? by when could it be achieved?). Various prioritisation tools can be helpful here (e.g. MoSCoW see page 20).

7. **Actions to take forward (will do)**
Discuss with the team that making every sail a +10 would make for an unbalanced boat: without anchors at all, stability might be reduced and direction compromised, so actions should be selected with this in mind. Invite the team to identify what actions should be taken, in what time frame and by whom. Make sure to continue to explore their thoughts and concerns as you complete this process with them. The boat can be revisited and even posted on the wall or electronically shared with the team members to remind them of the purpose mission and activity of the team.

Reference

Hohmann, L. (2006)
Innovation Games: Creating Breakthrough Products Through Collaborative Play.
Addison Wesley.

Maggie Grieve combines 30 years of global business-development leadership experience, team and executive coaching accreditations and her passion for facilitating lasting, positive change to help individuals and teams succeed and be happy in life and business.

SCARF

Ingredients

Pen and paper

Description

SCARF (Rock, 2008) is a brain-based model for collaborating with and influencing others. It may be applied and observed in any human interaction, whether at work, home or other social environment. It stands for Status, Certainty, Autonomy, Relatedness and Fairness – five experiential domains in group settings. 'Status' refers to an individual's relative professional or social standing. 'Certainty' refers to a belief that there is no rational reason to doubt our predictions of the immediate future. 'Autonomy' refers to an individual's capacity to make an informed, uncoerced decision and a sense of independent self-governance. 'Relatedness' refers to a desire to connect to and interact with others, and to experience caring for them and safety in their company. 'Fairness' refers to the subjective sensations of just and impartial exchanges without discrimination or favouritism. Its design has been drawn from a range of models including Maslow's Hierarchy of Needs (1981) and Self-Determination Theory (SDT) (Deci and Ryan, 1991).

When does it work best?

The SCARF model can help people manage themselves and others. They can recognise and reflect upon when their own domains are being threatened or rewarded by others and so root cause their emotional triggers. Similarly, having labelled the potential threat/reward impact of their own behaviours and interactions on others, they may choose to reappraise and modify such behaviours and interactions in ways that reward those domains in others. SCARF can be used when a client is having issues around how their behaviours are impacting on others or vice versa. For example, if a team member is feeling micromanaged on a particular project, it may threaten his autonomy and create significant anxiety. However, the manager may argue that she only micromanages because she needs more certainty around her inexperienced team member's ability to deliver on quality and quantity in a timely manner. Otherwise, it makes her anxious. Therefore, this example is an opportunity for the coach to discover with the client how both parties might work and develop together in a way that rewards their respective autonomy and certainty.

Step by step

1. Explain the model to the client in the coaching session, and why you've identified, from the issue, that SCARF may be relevant.
2. Ask the client to write down each domain.

SCARF

3. Ask the client to share examples of when, for them, each domain has been threatened and rewarded, how the subsequent feeling impacted upon them and what were the consequences.
4. Ask the client now to reflect on the issue presented for the session and how SCARF might be threatened and rewarded for both the client and for those with whom they're interacting.
5. As a result of the reflection, what behaviours would the client like to change in order to create desirable impact and consequences for all parties?
6. The client should write down their action plan and how they'll measure success.

Reference

Deci, E.L., and Ryan, R.M. (1991) *A Motivational Approach to Self: Integration in Personality.* pp.237–88.

Maslow, A.H. (1981) *Motivation and Personality.* Prabhat Prakashan.

Rock, D. (2008) SCARF: A Brain-based Model for Collaborating with and Influencing Others. *NeuroLeadership Journal*, 1(1): 44–52.

Callum O'Neill is a Henley coach specialising in executive, team and systems coaching, with a particular interest in double and triple loop learning.

STOKERS

Ingredients

None

When does it work best?

The technique can be used to start a coaching session and ensure the core components are used for contracting and goal setting. STOKERS works in a similar way to GROW or the ABCDE framework in cognitive-behavioural coaching, offering a clear, structured approach to each and every contracting session.

Description

STOKERS is a useful tool to help manage the first phase of the coaching conversation: contracting and goal setting. The tool was originally devised by Claire Pedrick (2020). The stoker is the person who shovels coal into the steam engine, while at the end of the journey the engine's fire is quelled with a second coaching tool: DOUSE (Foy, 2020) (see page 260). The tool is best used alongside a wider coaching contract, like PROMISE, developed by Karen Foy and Suzanne Hayes-Jones (Foy, 2020), which covers the way the coach and client will work together across the assignment.

It is worth noting that we need to revisit our commitment to confidentiality, with its exceptions, at the start of every session. These exceptions are likely to include, firstly, where there is serious criminality (for example, if the reporting of our 'crime' to the police would lead to a visit by a police officer within the following 48 hours and a possible arrest of the individual) and, secondly, where there is a serious risk of harm to the client or another individual. The most obvious example, perhaps, is where the client's emotional state means there is a serious risk of suicide or self-harm. In such cases, the coach may need to act (hopefully together with the client), contacting the appropriate services to ensure the client is safely in the care of others.

Step by step

1. Welcome the client to the session and, where appropriate, engage in small talk as you walk to the meeting room or remove a coat.
2. The STOKERS framework starts with the **S**ubject: "What would you like to focus on?" "What is the work you would like to consider today?"
3. **T**iming: "Given that we have 60 minutes today, what would be a good use of that time?" "In the time that we have, what part of that would you like to focus on?"
4. **O**utcome: "What would you like to have at the end of that time?" "What would make our time together successful?"
5. **K**nowledge: "How would you know you have that outcome?" "What would be different at the end of this session?"
6. **E**ssence: "What makes this important?"
7. **R**ole: "How can we best work together on this?" "What would you like from me as your coach?"
8. **S**tart: "Where would you like to start?"

References

Foy, K. (2020) Contracting in Coaching. In J. Passmore (ed.) *The Coaches' Handbook*. Abingdon: Routledge.

Pedrick, C. (2020) *Simplifying Coaching*. Maidenhead: McGraw-Hill Open University Press.

Karen Foy is a psychologist, an ICF accredited coach and trained supervisor, and a member of the Henley Centre for Coaching, Henley Business School.

DOUSE

Ingredients

None

Description

DOUSE is a useful tool to help manage closing a session and can be used nicely to follow STOKER (see page 259), which is a framework for managing the start of a coaching conversation. The stoker shovels coal into the steam engine, while at the end of the journey the engine's fire is quelled. The coach explores each step with the client through a specific question and uses follow-up questions at each stage, as required.

When does it work best?

The technique can be used to close a coaching session in partnership with the client.

Step by step

1. **D**ouble check – the coach starts to close by acknowledging that the conversation is coming towards an end and inviting their client to review the initial goals or plan set for the conversation.
2. **O**bstacles – the coach invites the client to think about any obstacles that might occur and prevent them from achieving their plan. (You can be an ally, here, or hold them to account.)
3. **U**ncovered – the aim of the third step is to reflect and enhance the client's learning and insight about themselves and their situation.
4. **S**upport – this step explores what support or resources the individual might need to achieve their plan.
5. **E**nding – the coach invites the client to close the session.

Karen Foy is a psychologist, an ICF accredited coach and trained supervisor, and a member of the Henley Centre for Coaching.

Suzanne Hayes-Jones is an ICF MCC accredited coach, coach mentor and coach supervisor.

Creator, Nurturer, Destroyer

Ingredients

None

Description

In Indian scripture, it is mentioned that there are three forces that are collectively controlling the world. These three forces are Brahma, Vishnu and Shiva. Brahma is the creator, Vishnu is the nurturer and Shiva is the destroyer. They keep working simultaneously to control the world. Brahma created the world, Vishnu nurtures it and Shiva destroys negativity whenever required. Using this framework, the coach invites their clients to explore their way of thinking, their assumptions, beliefs and so forth, and how these may be acting as barriers to goal achievement. Coaches also ask questions about clients' new thinking that might support the clients in their goal achievement and how these respective forces can be used to destroy, nurture or create new beliefs and assumptions.

Step by step

1. Ask the client if they have heard of Brahma, Vishnu and Shiva.
2. Briefly share with the client, in case they have not heard of Brahma, Vishnu and Shiva, their roles in the universe.
3. Explain that to reach a goal we sometimes need to nurture some assumptions or beliefs, destroy others and create new ones that reflect the changes the client hopes to achieve (their goals).
4. Explore which assumptions, beliefs, thinking and behavioural patterns may belong to the creation (new or add), nurture (strengthen) and destroyer (reduce or eliminate) categories respectively.
5. Remind the client of the dynamic nature of systems and the need for constant change.
6. Help the client, through reflection and discussion, to identify appropriate assumptions, beliefs, thinking and behavioural patterns to move closer to their goal.

Badri Bajaj is a leading coach, researcher, coaching trainer and ICF chapter president in India.

Six Thinking Hats

Ingredients

Paper of different colours cut in the shape of hats (optional)

Post-its (optional)

Description

This technique was developed by Edward de Bono (1985) to assess options from different angles/viewpoints. The client analyses the option using different lenses (hats), one at a time. The aim is that, by adopting these different perspectives, they will create a more rounded understanding of the issue. The technique can be used for both individual and team coaching.

Step by step

1. Explore the question in hand and develop a set of options without filters.
2. Once the options have been narrowed down, ask if they want to think about the options in an organised manner, then explain the basics of Six Thinking Hats.
3. Take out the paper hats (or labels) and set them in the centre of the table.
4. Use the blue hat to decide on a way forward: you can let them decide an order (which one they are most or least drawn to, the most challenging or comfortable one for them) or you as the coach can decide, based on what you have seen. A common place to start is the white hat.
5. With each hat, ask them to focus only on that specific mindset and to start enumerating everything that comes to mind without filtering out anything. For teams you can use Post-it notes for this part.
   - White hat: FACTS – What is the data available? What are past trends?
   - Red hat: FEELINGS – What does your intuition say, what is your gut reaction and emotions? How will other people react? In group settings, this can be done on a piece of paper: everybody votes and hands in their paper.
   - Black hat: NEGATIVES/CAUTIONS – Why might it not be a good option? What may go wrong? Why might proceeding with caution be recommended (dangers and difficulties)?
   - Yellow hat: GOOD POINTS – Positive aspects, optimistic outcomes, strengths, values and benefits.
   - Green hat: OPPORTUNITIES – Creative solutions/brainstorming. Free thinking with little criticism. What are the possibilities, alternatives and new ideas? New life.
   - Blue hat: PLANS – Process control or thinking more about the future.
6. Once they have exhausted their thoughts, ask them to introduce judgement and place that hat on the option it seems to favour.
7. Continue with the next hat until all hats are done.

When does it work best?

In one-to-one coaching, the tool can be used with individuals who need to assess choices, but who are not looking at the options from all angles. For team coaching, it can be used to explore options within a team, being specifically useful in helping teams to avoid groupthink or focusing on a narrow perspective. It can also be useful for groups to look at a situation from the same angle (e.g. all think about facts at the same time).

Six Thinking Hats

8. Ask questions about the exercise: how do they feel about the options now? Which colour do they normally favour most when making decisions? Are there any gaps in their knowledge? Are there any contingency plans that need to be prepared?
9. Close the activity when you feel they are ready, and set any necessary homework if any hats need to be explored further. For example, if there were few facts, maybe homework could be to research more about the subject.

Reference

de Bono, E. (1985) *Six Thinking Hats: An Essential Approach to Business Management*. Little, Brown & Company.

Claudia Day is an accredited coach and entrepreneur with a marketing strategy background, and trained in coaching at Henley Business School and management at MIT Sloan.

Sketching

Ingredients

Felt-tipped pens in a variety of colours

Sheets of plain paper (A4 or A3)

Pencils in a variety of colours

Pencil sharpener

Eraser

When does it work best?

Coaches often meet clients who are 'stuck for words'. Setting words aside and finding a visual way to present a topic can circumvent such blockages.

Description

Sketching has all the benefits associated with using visual imagery in coaching. In addition, the client is engaged in creating the image, meaning that it captures and represents the aspects that are most important to them. It taps into ways of seeing that talking alone does not reach, including the emotional content embodied in the topic being explored. Colours and abstract shapes can become powerful representations of a client's feelings about a subject that might otherwise be sensitive to talk about, or to find the words to express. Using the terms 'sketching' and 'doodling' helps to overcome negative perceptions some people can have about their ability to draw. When the sketch is a cartoon, the inclusion of humour can produce insights through the juxtaposition of unrelated ideas or the exposure of absurdities. Clients often find the sketches so powerful that they take them away, display them or use them with colleagues. They are certainly great aide memoires. In an alternative approach, the coach might take the role of visual rapporteur and capture the salient points in a sketch as the client talks things through. This can be a helpful approach when the client is absolutely stuck for where to start – they can always take over, once things are moving.

A client sketched his inner critic – a Dracula-type monster that could appear out of nowhere, sapping his energy and confidence. He explored the features and impact of this inner critical voice and then identified the aspects of the inner critic that might actually serve a useful purpose. In this way, the client was able to reimagine the inner voice as a critical friend.

Picture source: David Love

Sketching

References

Gash, J. (2017) Visual Processes. In *Coaching Creativity – Transforming Your Practice*. Abingdon: Routledge, Part V, Chapter 18, pp.155–66.

Schwarz, D., and Davidson, A. (2009) Starting with Yourself – Addressing Your Inner Critic. In *Facilitative Coaching – A Toolkit for Expanding Your Repertoire and Achieving Lasting Results*. San Francisco, CA: Pfeiffer, Chapter 4.

Sheather, A. (2019) *Coaching Beyond Words – Using Art to Deepen and Enrich Our Conversations*. Abingdon: Routledge. See also Anna's 'Art in Coaching' website.

Sibbert, D. (2013) Part 1 – The Visual Leadership Advantage. In *Visual Leaders – New Tools for Visioning, Management and Organization Change*. USA: The Grove Consultants International.

David Love is an executive coach and supervisor, working with public service leaders. He also teaches on Henley Business School's coaching programme.

Step by step

1. Invite your client to produce a sketch that depicts the core features of the topic they wish to explore. A starting point for a sketch might be a metaphor that the client has used (e.g. "It's like wading through treacle…").

2. If they are happy to do so, encourage them to give a running commentary about their sketching. Some clients, of course, will wish to remain silent as they work.

3. Invite the client to 'think like a cartoonist' in order to isolate the key characteristics needing to be illustrated and to introduce some humorous juxtapositions. Stick figures, lines, simple facial expressions and basic shapes can all be pressed into service in producing the sketch. Encourage them to keep words to a minimum, limiting these to succinct speech or thought bubbles and captions.

4. Throughout the process, notice how your client responds, invite reflection and enable them to mine their metaphors for insights.

5. Be appreciative and encouraging about the creation of the sketch. The 'technical' representation is irrelevant as long as the sketch makes sense to the client. Invite your client to go wild with off-the-wall possibilities – the kernel of an interesting idea can be lurking in the craziness.

6. Once the client has completed their sketch, invite them to talk about what they have depicted, the significance of the whole and of its constituent features. Focus in on factors such as figures and objects, and their juxtaposition. An exploration of shape, colour, texture and the sequence in which the sketch was produced can also prove fruitful in generating insights. Often, the process of producing the sketch is revelatory in some way – perhaps in giving validation to some strong feelings or in developing a greater understanding of the driving forces in a situation.

7. Ensure that the client's attention remains focused on their coaching goal and enable them to identify the insights and learning from the process.

SPIRE

Ingredients

Pen(s)

Paper

Whiteboard or flipchart

When does it work best?

This model works best when clients need to build more meaning in their work and/or have lost a sense of meaning (or engagement) at work during a period of change. It can also work well with clients who feel stuck in their current role and need to refresh their approach at work.

Reference

Steger, M. (2017) Creating Meaning and Purpose at Work. In Oades, L.G., Stege, M.F., Fave, A.D., and Passmore, J. (eds) *The Wiley-Blackwell Handbook of the Psychology of Positivity and Strengths-Based Approaches at Work*. Oxford: Wiley-Blackwell, pp.60–81.

Description

SPIRE is a model that can help people to create meaning and purpose at work. The model focuses on five potentially important levers for building meaningful work. The term 'SPIRE' is an acronym derived from the first letter of five factors: strengths, personalisation, integration, resonance and expansion. This model was based on the theoretical and empirical predictors of meaningful work, developed by Michael Steger (Steger, 2017), who proposed that the levers (factors) of this model can help identify pathways for more meaning at work:

Strengths: for example, knowing and levering your strengths, even if this is beyond what your job or role requires.

Personalisation: for example, bringing yourself to work, aligning your work with your values and taking personal ownership.

Integration: for example, integrating your motivation, and the way that you work, with other elements of your life.

Resonance: for example, understanding the broader organisational values and finding ways in which these will resonate with your own personal goals and meaning.

Expansion: for example, expanding your perspectives to things beyond yourself.

Step by step

1. Explain the model, listing the five key levers on a piece of paper, whiteboard or flipchart.
2. Invite the client to choose one of the key levers that stands out for them now.
3. Discuss this lever in depth – for example, by asking: "What does this mean here and now?" "What is working now for you here?" "What would you like to change in this area?" "What would it look, feel and sound like if the client were making this change at work?"
4. Ask the client to capture any notes or key insights on the paper, whiteboard or flipchart.
5. Working on the remaining four key levers, ask the client to choose another lever and discuss this in depth (as in step 3 or bringing new questions in).
6. When all levers have been discussed, ask the client to select (by circling or highlighting) 1–3 things that were captured by notes or key insights and that stand out for them now.
7. Discuss what they will do differently, within the next few weeks or so, to bring these to life at work.

Deb McEwen is an experienced accredited coach who has held senior leadership roles (NZ, AU and UK) and has an extensive background in health and wellbeing.

STARS

Ingredients

Post-it notes

Pens

Flipcharts (or optional digital whiteboard)

Big sunshine template (transformation roadmap) to go on the wall (or digital whiteboard)

When does it work best?

This technique works best at the start of a transformation programme, prior to any wider communications being sent, to enable the leadership team to build a joint vision and start to form a guiding coalition to lead the change. For team-building purposes, an off-site venue is recommended where possible. Online can work well with an external facilitator and a technical platform that allows online presentations, a shared whiteboard and breakout rooms.

Description

STARS is a creational tool that can be used in a number of ways to help support successful organisational transformation. It can be used as a diagnostic tool during individual coaching sessions with leaders of transformation to identify areas for improvement, but it is best used in a workshop environment with a leadership team to envision the future and create a transformation roadmap. The term 'STARS' is an acronym derived from five interlinked areas – **s**trategy, **t**alent, **a**nalytics, **r**elationships and **s**ystems – that need to be understood, planned and aligned at each stage of a transformation process, which is where your coaching skills come in.

- **Strategy** – What is the strategy for your department and how does this contribute to the overarching objectives for your organisation? How well does this align to your vision and values? What objectives do you need to achieve, 12 months from now, to deliver this? 18 months? 24? Articulate your vision in one sentence to describe what the future looks like once this has been achieved.
- **Talent** – What capabilities (skills, knowledge and behaviours) are required to deliver against that strategy? How do these compare with the existing capability within your team? What is your plan to move people from where they are now to where they need to be?
- **Analytics** – What data and information will you need to measure the performance of your department and what do your people need to be successful? How much of that is available today? How will you develop a baseline measure so you can monitor changes during the transformation period? What does success look like?
- **Relationships** – What relationships exist between your department and other areas? Consider inter-team relationships, inter-departmental relationships and external relationships with customers, suppliers and partners. How well are these working today? Are there any blockers? Do you trust each other? What needs to change and what needs to be maintained?
- **Systems** – What existing systems and processes do you have? How do these support your people to deliver the objectives you want to achieve? What might need to change? How could you make them even better? What else is required to generate the information and data you need as efficiently as possible?

Step by step

1. Explain the model to the client in a one-to-one coaching session and explore it from three time frames: before, now (as is) and the future (to be).
2. If the 'as is' is understood, then suggest a workshop to explore and design the 'to be', as a leadership team. If not, suggest the client undertakes some discovery work first.
3. Issue some pre-work to the leadership team that includes an agenda, the STARS model and a request for them to consider what they might like to include under each area. Activities to prompt thinking can include: looking outside of their industry to get a sense of best practice, thinking about what has worked well in previous organisations and identifying problem areas they would like to address through the transformation. This can be done with the senior leadership team only, but should include the extended leadership team where possible.
4. On the day: use your favourite ice-breaker and then get the leader to set some context and get people fired up about the opportunity the transformation brings.
5. As a collective, agree a single vision statement of what the future will look and feel like when the strategy is achieved. Or, if working with a large group, break out into small groups, devise one each and then come back to agree a single vision statement as a team.
6. Get them to write the agreed vision statement, word for word, in the topic area (the sun) of the 'Sun Ray' chart. The rays will be labelled: 'Talent', 'Analytics', 'Relationships' and 'Systems'.
7. Divide into four teams to explore the remaining element of the STARS model in the context of the agreed strategy.
8. Each sub-team is tasked with a time-machine review of its area. For example, "if you chose 'Technology', jump in your time machine together, step out 5 years from now, take a look around and describe how technology is supporting your department." Get them to flipchart the answers. Part 1 is a brainstorm: individuals add Post-it notes of ideas to the flipchart, and there's no such thing as a silly idea. Part 2 is to agree the art of the possible. What elements make people think 'what if'? Can the Post-it notes be clustered into themes?
9. Teams present back the identified themes to each other and, through facilitated discussion, get a sense of what might be.
10. As a final exercise, get each team to add its vision of the final year on the sunshine chart and to add 3–5 things that need to happen the year before to get there, and the year before that again, using Post-it notes and clustering technique.
11. To close, get commitment from each sub-team to meet again and develop a detailed plan based on the output from the workshop. These should be collated by an agreed central person and the completed sunshine chart should be reviewed, agreed and signed-off as the transformation roadmap.

Christine Lithgow Smith is an experienced senior leader and founder of Chrisalyst®, and is now completing doctoral research into leadership awareness.

Using Sticky Notes

Ingredients

Sticky notes in a variety of colours

Thick felt-tipped pens in a variety of colours

Flipchart or paper

When does it work best?

This technique works best when the client is faced with complexity, involving a diverse range of systemic factors, people and emotions. Clients typically find sticky notes helpful for unpacking complicated tasks, challenges or successes.

Reference

Gash, J. (2017) Visual Processes. In *Coaching Creativity – Transforming Your Practice*. Abingdon: Routledge, Part V, Chapter 18, pp.155–66.

David Love is an executive coach and supervisor, working with public service leaders. He also teaches on Henley Business School's coaching programme.

Description

Using sticky notes in coaching is a simple way to help a client bring to the fore and organise their thoughts and ideas. They are a great way to capture the key elements of a situation and make them visible to the client, making them graspable in a way that would not be possible through talking alone. Sticky notes can be clustered (and re-clustered), allowing the client to see and make connections. The physicality of moving the notes around often helps the client with their thinking and analysis. Different-coloured sticky notes and/or pens can be used to differentiate the various elements involved, such as the range of forces and drivers, the helping and hindering factors, and the emotions at play. How the client *feels* can often be far more important than the facts.

Step by step

1. Decide who will do the writing. If the client writes, they will capture the points they believe to be the most salient. Conversely, if the coach writes, the client is freed up to think and reflect. Of course, the coach must then capture the main points accurately – and in the client's words. In the steps below, the coach is the scribe.
2. As the client opens up about their topic, capture the key points. Notice and signpost the emotional elements along with the facts. Prompt the client, encouraging them to explore the topic as broadly and deeply as possible so that a rich picture is established on the sticky notes.
3. When the client believes they have finished, challenge them to produce more points – there will invariably be more to emerge.
4. Ask the client to notice and comment on any themes or sub-themes emerging during the previous step. Different-coloured sticky notes or pens can be used to differentiate them. What connections and patterns can they see? Encourage them to cluster the sticky notes in ways that make sense to them.
5. Ensure the client's exploration is not superficial, to enable them to check the detailed thinking behind the clusters, to challenge their perceptions and assumptions, and to draw attention to the emerging learning points and insights. Depending on the complexity of the topic, there may be a number of clusterings or re-clusterings undertaken by the client before they gain a deeper understanding of the situation and are then able to work on ways forward.
6. Clients often like to keep a record of their explorations. Invite them to photograph the sticky-note clusters.

STOP

Ingredients

None

When does it work best?

The technique works best when a client is caught up by emotion or struggling to disentangle themselves from negative thoughts, feelings or sensations. By working through a gentle process, allowing for pauses, it encourages a mindful state to reflect and then act in accordance with their values.

Description

The STOP technique was developed by Joseph Ciarrochi, Ann Bailey and Russ Harris (Ciarrochi et al., 2015) to encourage a mindful pause when making decisions and considering choices. This technique is used within the Acceptance and Commitment Therapy (ACT) model (Hayes, 2019) and allows the client to ground themselves in times of crisis, bringing them into the present moment. The term is an acronym that allows the coach to guide the client through a step-by-step process: **s**low your breathing, **t**ake note, **o**pen up and **p**ursue values. A crisis for the client could present or manifest in many ways that include emotions or difficulty separating from tricky thoughts, feelings or sensations. The technique is a useful tool, particularly when the client can't see the wood for the trees or their crisis is all consuming. The STOP process is used with the client as follows:

Slow down – slowing their breath takes the client to a place of calm, allowing them to be in the present moment;

Take note – noticing their breath, thoughts, feelings and the sensations within their body;

Open up – make room and create space for their thoughts, feelings and bodily sensations;

Pursue value – allowing the client to consider who they want to be, how they act and whether it aligns to their personal values. Finally, create one small action step.

Step by step

1. Explain the technique and seek permission to explore.
2. Ask the client to take a moment to **slow down** and to start to focus on their breathing. Invite the client to take a deep breath in for three seconds, pause for four seconds and release for five seconds, then pause again and repeat the process until a natural breathing rhythm is found.
3. Ask the client to take a moment to just **take note**, noticing and becoming aware of each in-breath and out-breath. Invite them to notice their thoughts, their feelings and any sensations in their body (e.g. tension in their shoulders, a knot in their stomach, etc.). Clarify that this part of the exercise is purely just to notice, not to pass judgement or to try to change these factors.
4. Create the time and the space to allow the client to **open up** around their thoughts, feelings and sensations. Ask the client to use their breath to observe and acknowledge what is going on for them. They should not dismiss these feelings, but simply observe them. The body of the client is the container in this process, which doesn't need to involve the coach in the dialogue.

STOP

5. Invite the client to **pursue their values** by asking them to consider the following questions: "How do I want to respond, show up or conduct myself in this crisis?" "What do I stand for?" "How would I like to act?"
6. Get the client to consider one small action step to move forward.

References

Ciarrochi, J., Harris, R., and Bailey, A. (2015) *The Weight Escape: Stop Fad Dieting, Start Losing Weight and Reshape Your Life Using Cutting-edge Psychology*. UK: Hachette.

Hayes, S. (2019) *A Liberated Mind: The Essential Guide to ACT*. London: Random House.

Viki Rice is a Henley executive coach and is passionate about supporting clients to regain their confidence and find balance, enabling them to find space to take action and grow.

Strengths Bull's Eye

Ingredients

A large piece of paper and pens

When does it work best?

When leaders and managers would like to gain greater self-awareness and more versatility in their approach. It can also be adapted for working with teams, helping to understand diversity within the team, and the strengths and over-strengths of the team as a whole. This can help lead to team behaviour change and wider impacts within the system.

Julie Flower is a leadership and team development coach, consultant and facilitator, specialising in navigating uncertainty in complex systems and applied improvisation.

Description

A strengths bull's eye is a powerful and visual way for a client to explore both their strengths and their 'over-strengths'. An over-strength is a strength that we may use too much or inappropriately in certain settings. Whilst many people recognise the concept of strengths and may have strong self-awareness of these within the workplace, they may be less well aware of their over-strengths and how these manifest themselves. Sometimes, our greatest strengths can also be our greatest weaknesses. For instance, a strength of collaboration may become limiting if used in all situations, stymying decision-making and taking up significant amounts of time engaging stakeholders in issues that simply don't require significant collaborative work. Gaining an awareness of over-strengths can help leaders and managers adapt their style and guard against the potential pitfalls of overusing their strengths, whilst capitalising on the benefits of them.

Step by step

1. Ask the client to draw a large bull's eye (three concentric circles) on a piece of flipchart paper.
2. In the centre, ask them to identify some of their key strengths. If the client has never explored their strengths before, it may be helpful to use an online instrument or strengths cards/prompts to support them in identifying their strengths.
3. Working through each strength in turn, the client should list the corresponding behaviour or attribute that manifests itself as an over-strength – when the strength is taken too far. For instance, their strength of engagement may sometimes lead to exhaustion in situations where they over-engage.
4. During the coaching conversation, it is helpful to ask if they have specific examples or if they have received feedback from colleagues about their use of strengths and over-strengths. Encourage the client to consider the situations in which the strength serves them well and when it may become unhelpful to them, if overused or applied inappropriately.
5. In the outer circle, ask the client to note down modifying behaviours to help make the most of their strengths but guard against the pitfalls of over-strengths.
6. Encourage the client to experiment with and seek feedback on their new approaches. They should keep their strengths bull's eye visible and accessible, as a living document.

SUPER-POWER

Ingredients

None

When does it work best?

This technique works best in contexts where someone lacks confidence, struggles with Imposter Syndrome, or feels uncertain about their place or role, at work or in life. Knowing our individual super-power can become a strong, positive foundation for making choices around career and life transitions, as well as building self-confidence.

Description

When we think about developing ourselves, it can be all too easy to focus on our 'areas of improvement'. What if instead we focused on our unfair advantage? What if we explored what makes us unique and why people are drawn to us? What if we were able to understand the sweet spot of where our strengths combine with our core values to give us energy? Drawing on positive psychology principles, this coaching technique enables us to define the intersection of our individual strengths and our values. A series of short exercises enables us to uncover our unique 'super-power' where our values and strengths align and refine it into a succinct, memorable and empowering statement.

Step by step

This technique can be used as a condensed version of a single session of around one hour, or an extended version spread over three one-hour sessions:
- Session 1: steps 1 to 5, focusing on personal strengths;
- Session 2: steps 6 and 7, focusing on values;
- Session 3: steps 8 and 9, focusing on refinement and usage.

Options for exercises have been given for both the extended and condensed versions.

1. In advance of the session, discuss with the client how understanding our unique super-power can shine a light on our ideal role and place in a team, an organisation and in life, and can enhance our self-confidence. To gain insights and begin the reflection process, ask the client to prepare for the session in advance by reviewing any existing and current data points such as appraisals, 360 reviews and psychometrics.
    If the client does not have any existing data points, they should complete a couple of exercises before the session. For more concrete data, try the VIA strength finder online tool. For more anecdotal data, the client should ask five friends and/or colleagues, who know them well, the following question: what are the three things that make me unique? The client should ask themselves the same question and write their responses down.
    Whilst reviewing their data, the client should reflect on a couple of questions: what made you smile when you read it? What positive words and phrases stand out?
2. Work through the POWER U model. If it is useful, you can walk through an overview of the steps of the model with the client before you start the session, and refer to it to signpost to the client where you are during the process.

SUPER-POWER

3. **P**OSITION
To begin, we get an understanding of where we are starting from, focusing firmly on the individual's strengths. Ask the client to summarise their insights and reflections from reviewing their data points, highlighting only the positives and the strengths. As coach, listen out for and note all key words. What are the patterns? Where do you sense the client has energy? Where do you hear most impact? Share your observations with the client and repeat back key words and phrases. Gently pull the client back to focus on the positives if they stray into any negatives. Useful questions include:
   • What made you smile when you read it?
   • What surprised you? What resonated with you?
   • What positive words and phrases do you see? What strengths do you see?
   • What patterns do you see?
4. **O**NLY ME
The next step is to zoom in on the strengths that are most unique and important to the individual. The aim is for the client to select their two most important unique strengths. Be sure to acknowledge the breadth of strengths the client has. Useful questions include:
   • Which of these strengths resonate most with you?
   • What is unique to you?
   • What is your unfair advantage? What makes people come to you for something over anyone else?
   • From all the strengths you have, which two are the most important to you?
5. **W**HY
In this step, we explore what motivates the client in terms of their values. Briefly discuss with the client their understanding of values, exploring the idea that when the things that we do and the way we behave match our values, we tend to feel satisfied and content. There are a couple of methods to explore values: which one you choose will depend on the time you have available.
Condensed version: use a pre-made list of suggested values (for example, VIA) and ask the client to highlight all those that feel important to them. Ask the client to use their intuition to move quite quickly through the list, adding any that have meaning for them and are not listed. Next, ask them to review the list and put a second mark against their top five values. Rank them to get the top priority. Check the priority feels correct and highlight the top two.

SUPER-POWER

Extended session: take a plain piece of paper or virtual whiteboard and ask the client to draw a timeline across the page or screen from birth to the current day. Identify and draw above the line the three moments when life felt just right and in the flow. Identify and draw below the line three moments when they felt blocked, empty or frustrated. Ask the client to briefly tell the story of each. For the moments above the line, ask questions around:

- What made it special?
- What triggered the feelings of fulfilment?
- What did this mean for you?

For the moments below the line, ask them questions around:

- What made these moments feel bad?
- What was being ignored, trampled on or not honoured at these times?

Record and summarise back the words that were repeated, where you felt the client had most energy and impact. Ask the client to use these words and make them into a list, phrasing them as positive values. Check-in with the client that each value resonates and keep checking that the language fits. Ask the client to rank their list. Check the priority feels correct and highlight the top two.

Be sure to write the values in positive language, for example transform 'not failing' into 'being successful'.

6. **E**NERGY

You now have a list of the client's top-two strengths and top-two values. Draw a two-circle Venn diagram, with a large S in the segment where they intersect. Ask the client to write their two strengths in the left-hand circle and their two values in the right-hand one. Sense check that the strengths and values are right and fit the client. Useful questions here include:

- How does this feel? Is this you?
- What would you like to change?
- What else needs to change?

7. **R**EFINE

Now we pull together the strengths and values to find where they intersect: the sweet spot in the centre is the client's unique super-power. Ask the client to refine the strengths and values they have identified into a short, memorable phrase – the more concise the better. Sense check that it is the correct summary of the client's super-power. Useful questions here include:

- If we were to combine your strengths and weaknesses into a short phrase that sums you up, what would it be?
- Imagine your superhero cape, emblazoned with your super-power phrase on the back. Try it on. Say it out loud a few times. How does it fit?
- What would you like to change in the phrase? What would make it fit even better?

SUPER-POWER

8. **U**SE

We close the session by embedding the notion of the super-power and supporting the client to action-plan how their super-power will be most useful to them, moving forwards. Useful questions include:

- What has been the most insightful element of the exercise?
- Now that you know you have this super-power, how will you use it?
- When can you imagine knowing your super-power will be most useful to you?
- What will you do to remember your super-power?

Claire Finch supports individuals and teams to believe in themselves by unlocking their energy, so they can achieve their business and personal potential.

Disney Strategy – Three Thinking Hats

Ingredients

Space to move around

For groups, Post-its can be used

When does it work best?

The technique works best in complex situations where the client does not know the best way forward and there would be value on thinking creatively about it.

Description

This technique was developed by Robert Dilts (1995). It allows the person to think creatively by providing a space for being a dreamer, a realist and a critic. It can be used in a variety of contexts. This model works in a sequence, starting with the dreamer phase, which is a generative stage with no concerns about practicality or possibility. If anything were possible, what would the option be? Once the creativity has been exhausted, this is given to the realist, who then tries to convert these ideas into practical and feasible solutions asking "how could…?" and coming up with realistic proposals, thinking about applications of the ideas, action plans, timelines and resources needed. Finally, this is given to the critic, who evaluates the ideas. While using the critic hat, the aim is to give both positive and negative feedback in a constructive manner, looking at all the potential roadblocks, limitations and weaknesses.

After going through the cycle once, the cycle can be repeated as many times as is considered necessary. The goal is for the client first to think about it without any restrictions. It works as a funnel. Start with the dreamer, to brainstorm as many ideas as possible. Be cautious to really exhaust all options, then introduce the realist and the critic, subsequently. This will automatically narrow down the ideas. There is a slight variation to this exercise that includes a spectator's view. This can be any stakeholder or an observer or consultant. For this stage, the aim is to provide facts and data, not opinions. These can be introduced for a second cycle.

Step by step

1. Ask the client if they have heard of the Disney Strategy.
2. Share with them the aim of the activity – to think about the topic first as a dreamer, then as a realist and finally as a critic.
3. Have them choose three spaces that feel right. For example, some people might choose the window as the place of the dreamer and the door as the place for the realist. They may also find it useful to think of roles, characters or people they find are dreamers, realists and critics (e.g. Mandela, Mary Poppins, my dad, my boss, accountants, a worker at IDEO, myself when I was doing X project).

Dreamer	Realist	Critic
What comes to mind? (Do not let any filters come in. Exhaust the list.) Why is this important to you and to others? (Exhaust all reasons, from different perspectives, e.g. values, money, relationship. You can use the wheel of life to see what it impacts.) How will you know that you have achieved what you wanted? How will you feel? What does it look like? What is happening around you? Is there a role model to follow? Are there previous instances when this happened that would make you think differently about it? If you step back to see it as a whole, does it look different?	What do you see yourself doing and how would you implement it? (Exhaust all possible alternatives.) How will you know the goal has been achieved? What are the steps to get there? What does your gut tell you? If you step back to see it as a whole, does it look different?	What are you hesitant about? Why? (Exhaust all hesitations.) Thinking long term, what are your thoughts? Thinking only short term, what are your thoughts? What other facts would you need to understand better? If you step back to see it as a whole, does it look different? If you zoom in and look at the detail, does it look different? What are the strengths and weaknesses?

In group coaching, the dream stage could be done with Post-its, where each of the members puts their ideas and then shares them with the group. The realist and critic can be then assessed as a team, all together.

4. After going step by step through the process, ask the client if they want to go through the cycle again. Do it as many times as the client feels is beneficial. For teams, there may be value in doing a second cycle because new ideas might arise inspired from seeing the other members' ideas.

5. Ask the client about takeaways and next steps, which may include researching facts, doing testing and so forth (Bossons et al., 2009; Evatt et al., 2002).

References

Bossons, P., Kourdi, J., and Sartain, D. (2009) Coaching: Practical, Proven Techniques for World-class Executive Coaching. London: A.&C. Black.

Dilts, R. (1995) *Strategies of Genius*. Capitola, CA: Meta Publications.

Evatt, M.A.C., Design Conference, National Conference on Product Design Education (eds) (2002) Sharing Experience in Engineering Design: Proceedings of the 24th SEED Annual Design Conference and 9th National Conference on Product Design Education, 3–4 September 2002, Coventry University, Coventry, UK. Presented at the SEED Annual Design Conference, Professional Engineering Publ, Bury St Edmunds.

Claudia Day is an accredited coach and entrepreneur with a marketing strategy background and trained in coaching at Henley Business School and management at MIT Sloan.

What's in Your Rucksack?

Ingredients

Ten or so sheets of paper – blank or with the outline of a rock

Description

Clients are often weighed down by assumptions, past issues and future concerns. This technique invites the client to imagine they are on a journey and have a large rucksack. It's very heavy and is making their journey hard. Through a coaching conversation, the client is encouraged to look inside their rucksack and describe what the various heavy items (rocks) are in it that they are carrying around. Each one is written down on a separate sheet of paper. When the client feels that they have emptied the rucksack, they are asked what they want do with each of the 'rocks'. If they feel able to, they can scrunch them up and symbolically throw them away. If they are not ready to let a rock go, they can decide to put it back in the rucksack for now, but should remember that it is there so that they can take it back out later and see whether it really should be there. The key point is not to expect that all the rocks can just disappear – that will take time – but knowing what they are and that they are still being carried around is a big step towards reducing the weight in the metaphorical rucksack.

Step by step

1. Ask the client to imagine that they are on a long walk. It's a hot day and they are getting tired. They have on a heavy rucksack. Get them to describe what it looks like.
2. They come to a bench – perhaps overlooking a lake. Again, ask them to describe where they are.
3. The coach is already sitting on the bench and they get into a conversation. The client mentions the weight of the rucksack.
4. The coach asks what is in the rucksack – and whether they would be prepared to look inside.
5. Using the sheets of paper, the client writes down what each of the rocks in the rucksack represents.
6. Keep going until they either feel they have emptied the rucksack or have identified that there are rocks in there they still don't recognise. That's OK – there is no pressure to get the rucksack completely empty.
7. The client then examines each sheet of paper in turn and describes a bit more about what the rock represents and how heavy it is in the rucksack. They then indicate whether they are able to put it down on the bench, to put it back in the rucksack or to get rid of it.
8. If there are any rocks left on the bench, go back at the end to see whether they want to put them back for now – or remove them.
9. Ask the client how heavy the rucksack feels now and how they are going to make sure the rocks they removed don't find their way back in.
10. Suggest a follow-up session at a later date to revisit this, to see whether any more rocks can be removed – or whether some are still there, despite having thought that they'd gone…

Calum Byers has over 30 years' senior line-management experience and is now a Henley-trained, ICF-credentialled executive coach.

Wheel of Work

Ingredients

Paper and pen

When does it work best?

The tool works best for junior or middle managers, for those recently in a new role or who may be considering a move to a new role.

Description

Like the 'Wheel of Life', the 'Wheel of Work' tool provides an opportunity for clients to reflect on their current role and the balance between the various components through the use of a wheel and ratings. It can be used in several ways (Bird and Gornall, 2016).

Step by step

1. Ask the client if they would like to look at their job in a more granular way.
2. Invite them to consider what is important for them in a role, and to label the categories:
   a. Being motivated – Motivation
   b. Creating a lasting impact – Impact
   c. Getting financial recognition – Salary
   d. Feeling work and life are in balance – Wellbeing
   e. Being supported by colleagues – Support
   f. Having enough freedom to make decisions – Autonomy
   g. Having friendships at work – Relationships
   h. Growing as a professional – Professional Development.
3. Label the sections on their wheel:

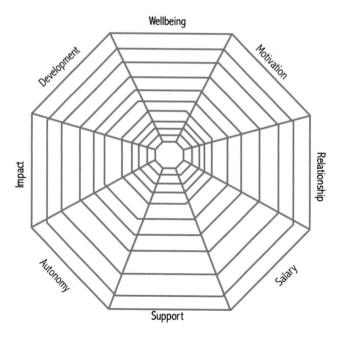

Wheel of Work

4. Invite the client to rate their current role on a scale of 1–10.
5. Explore these ratings with the client:
    a. Which areas fulfil you the most? Why? What are the consequences?
    b. Which areas are you most uncertain of or dissatisfied about? Why? What are the consequences?
    c. How do you feel when you look at the wheel? What comes to mind? Exhaust everything that comes to mind.
    d. Reflect on each area. What are the positive experiences with each? How have you impacted each, both positively and negatively?
    e. What are your goals for each area? What would you like to change/develop and why?
    f. Are there any conflicts between them?
    g. What does this tell you about yourself?
6. What needs to change based on your answers? What would an action plan look like?
7. Continue the coaching as you would normally do.

Reference

Bird, J., and Gornall, S. (2016) *The Art of Coaching: A Handbook of Tips and Tools*. Abingdon: Routledge.

Claudia Day is an accredited coach and entrepreneur with a marketing strategy background, and trained in coaching at Henley Business School and management at MIT Sloan.

Using Visual Images

Ingredients

A pack of coloured photographs

Description

Visual images, as advertisers know, have a powerful emotional impact on people – so introducing pictures into a coaching conversation can be a very effective way of encouraging important feelings to be surfaced and their impacts to be explored. At a fundamental level, visual images simply offer a novel way of looking at a topic. Clients are clever, resourceful people who will have thought about their topic before connecting up with a coach. Using pictures immediately throws things into a new arena and the stronger connection with the emotional elements involved leads to greater insight – often into the important factors that underpin the more obvious features of a topic. Clients often make strong connection with the pictures themselves. They become a metaphor, and therefore a 'language', to use in exploring their topic.

When does it work best?

Pictures provide a stimulating way to enable clients to see things from new and different angles. They can be particularly helpful when a client is stuck and cannot see a way past the obstacles. Visual images tap into the emotional elements of a situation and so can be helpful in encouraging a different perspective that moves the client out of a purely cognitive and rational way of looking at things. There are many ways to use pictures: one way is for the client to use them to establish the present state and desired future for a challenge they are facing.

Step by step

1. Lay out the images and invite the client to select three pictures that speak to them in some way about the topic they have brought to coaching.
2. Ask them to outline the reasons for their choices. Often clients make very clear linkages between their topic (or an aspect of it) and the images, and gain a greater understanding as a result of the perceptions being offered from a different viewpoint. Encourage an in-depth examination of the metaphor(s) the client is using when explaining the connections between their topic and the pictures.
3. Notice, and explore, how your client is responding to, and working with, the images.
4. Sometimes, the client will choose pictures very quickly. On other occasions, they may need a little time. Exploring the reasons behind the speed of their decision-making can unearth some additional pertinent thinking.

Using Visual Images

5. Draw attention to the feelings the client has about the images and their relationship with their topic to help deepen their understanding of the emotional factors at play.
6. Offer constructive challenge about the client's assumptions and encourage them to highlight the emerging learning and insights. What light do these throw on their goal for the coaching conversation?
7. If appropriate, repeat the process with images selected for their connections to a desired future state.
8. With the present and future states fully explored, invite the client to undertake a gap analysis as the starting point for working through how to move progressively towards the desired resolution.
9. Invite the client to take photographs of their chosen images for future reference.

References

Gash, J. (2017) Visual Processes. In *Coaching Creativity – Transforming Your Practice*. Abingdon: Routledge, Part V, Chapter 18, pp.155–66.

Housden, C. (undated) *Liminal Muse Cards*. charlottehousden.com.

Schwarz, D., and Davidson, A. (2009) Making it Visual. In *Facilitative Coaching – A Toolkit for Expanding Your Repertoire and Achieving Lasting Results*. San Francisco, CA: Pfeiffer, Chapter 8.

David Love is an executive coach and supervisor, working with public service leaders. He also teaches on Henley Business School's coaching programme.

Benefit Finding

Ingredients

None

When does it work best?

The tool is specifically focused towards helping clients who have experienced traumatic events. In coaching terms, this may be redundancy or dismissal, either for the individual or for members of their team.

Reference

Affleck, G., and Tennen, H. (1996) Construing Benefits from Adversity: Adaptational Significance and Dispositional Underpinnings. *Journal of Personality*, 64, 899–922.

Jonathan Passmore is a chartered psychologist, accredited coach, supervisor and director of the Henley Centre for Coaching, Henley Business School.

Description

Finding positives from a traumatic event, such as redundancy or dismissal, can help clients manage during what is often a stressful and difficult time. For instance, understanding that challenging life events can be beneficial has been shown to enhance resilience, spirituality, relationship strength and compassion, and to create a new sense of purpose (Affleck and Tennen, 1996). This tool draws on positive psychological research findings to help clients to direct their thinking towards a recognition that all events contain both positive and negative aspects. How we experience them depends on us. As with a number of tools in this book, coaches need to be careful not to step beyond the boundaries of their competence or their qualifications. Most coaches are not trained therapists or psychologists, and do not have special training with trauma management. In such cases, such as post-traumatic stress disorder (PTSD) or where a clinical condition such as depression is involved, the coach should refer the client to a specialist or wait until the client is capable of engaging in a coaching relationship.

Step by step

1. The client may have approached the coach specifically to discuss the event or been referred by their organisation, sometimes as part of a package to support those under-going redundancy.
2. The coach should invite the client to talk about the traumatic event. During this step, allowing space for the client to talk, while empathetically listening, enables to client to share their story and to express their feelings for a few minutes. This may last 15 minutes, or the whole two hours of the session.
3. On completion of this step, once it is appropriate, the coach can invite the client to consider possible positive aspects of the experience. The practitioner may guide this step by asking questions such as:
   - "What has the experience taught you?"
   - "How has the experience made you better equipped to meet similar challenges in the future?"
   - "If a friend was going through the same experience, how would you be able to support them?"
4. Care needs to be taken not to rush the client to step 3, or to trivialise the client's situation with *"come on now, sunny side up"* thinking. Instead, the aim is to encourage clients to recognise that every situation may have positives, even though these may be outweighed in the short term by negatives.

Using Hope Theory

Ingredients

None

Description

Hope Theory can be very valuable during coaching conversations. Theorists have suggested that human behaviour is largely goal directed (Rand and Cheavens, 2009). With that in mind, hope is defined as "goal directed thinking" (Lopez, Pedrotti and Snyder, 2015: 204) that brings together two key elements that are relevant to coaching: Pathways thinking (the ability to imagine possible routes towards a desired goal) and Agency thinking (the necessary motivation to pursue those routes) (Lopez, Pedrotti and Snyder, 2015). Using Hope Theory in coaching involves supporting clients to make strong connections between an imagined, attractive future and a perceived current state (van Nieuwerburgh and Love, 2019). According to two leading theorists in this field, there are a number of ways to enhance Pathways and Agency thinking: breaking long-term goals into smaller steps; rehearsing scripts and strategies needed to overcome any hurdles; recalling past successes in achieving goals; identifying secondary goals if the original goal is blocked; and enjoying the process of working towards goals (Magyar-Moe and Lopez, 2015). The role of the coach is to increase hopefulness by using some of the strategies listed below.

When does it work best?

Using Hope Theory works best when the client is doubting their ability to achieve certain goals. The strategies proposed below can increase self-belief and a sense of self-efficacy, increasing the chances of success for the client.

Step by step

1. Initially, the coach can support the client by helping them to identify existing resources. For example, "what is already in place to help you to achieve this goal?"
2. The coach should also listen out for skills that the client already has, reflecting these back to the client to increase their self-belief. For example, "It sounds like you are a good problem-solver."
3. Asking about past successes can also build a sense of self-efficacy. For example, "Can you think of a time that you have overcome a similarly challenging situation?"
4. Normalising the situation is also helpful. In other words, the coach can share information that helps the client to realise that they are not alone in encountering certain challenges. For example, "I've heard that many organisations are experiencing something quite similar."

Using Hope Theory

References

Lopez, S., Pedrotti, J., and Snyder, C. (2015) *Positive Psychology: The Scientific and Practical Explorations of Human Strengths* (3rd edition). Thousand Oaks, CA: Sage.

Magyar-Moe, J., and Lopez, S. (2015) Strategies for Accentuating Hope. In S. Joseph (ed.), *Positive Psychology in Practice: Promoting Human Flourishing in Work, Health, Education, and Everyday Life* (2nd edition). Chichester: Wiley, pp.483–502.

Rand, K. L., & Cheavens, J. S. (2009) Hope theory. In S. J. Lopez & C. R. Snyder (Eds.), *Oxford library of psychology. Oxford handbook of positive psychology* (p. 323–333). Oxford University Press.

van Nieuwerburgh, C., and Love, D. (2019) *Advanced Coaching Practice: Inspiring Change in Others*. London: Sage.

Dr Christian van Nieuwerburgh is Professor of Coaching and Positive Psychology, University of East London and Executive Director of Growth Coaching International.

David Love is an executive coach and supervisor, working with public service leaders. He also teaches on Henley Business School's coaching programme.

5. During the options stage, encouraging creativity can be very helpful for the client. The coach's aim is to increase the number of possible ways forward in order to support the client to feel that they have numerous options.

6. Finally, asking the client to imagine a future situation when they have overcome the challenges can increase positivity and motivation. For example, "What will your work life be like if you achieve this goal?" When the client responds, the coach should ask for more detailed information so that the client can immerse themselves in that positive future.

Sky and Weather

Ingredients

Image of the sky

When does it work best?

The technique works best for clients within an ACT framework, where the client is struggling to manage unhelpful, negative or illogical thinking. Rather than encourage the client to dispute the thinking through a more evidenced-based perspective, ACT encourages the client to recognise that these thoughts are not the truth, they are not part of who they are as a person: the client has the choice to ignore these thoughts and to move on to more productive thinking.

Description

This technique is drawn from an original idea developed by a Buddhist writer (Chodron, 1997) but it fits nicely with Acceptance and Commitment coaching, and like many ACT techniques uses a metaphor to help the client to reframe their thinking about an issue (Harris, 2009). Like 'Leaves on a Stream', this technique aims to help clients to recognise they are not their thoughts, in the same way that the weather is not the sky. The sky is so much bigger and constant (or at least only slowly changing) while the weather changes from hour to hour, day to day and season to season.

Step by step

1. The client may express their unhelpful thought: "*This has been a dreadful week, there is so much to do at work. I can't get through it.*"
2. Describe the metaphor: sky and weather. "*While the weather may change, the sky remains constant. We may see the weather in the sky, but they are different. Today, it's raining. Tomorrow may be windy. By the weekend it could be sunny. In what ways is your thinking similar to this situation?*"
3. Help the client to explore how our mood and emotions may change, but these emotions do not define who we are. They are the weather. Help the client to find their own umbrella for the rainy days, a coat for cold days and sun cream for sunny days, while recognising that neither the sun nor the rain defines who they are.

References

Chodron, P. (1997) *When Things Fall Apart: Heart Advice for Difficult Times*. Boulder, CO: Shambhala.

Harris, R. (2009) *ACT Made Simple*. Oakland, CA: New Harbinger Publications, Inc.

Jonathan Passmore is a chartered psychologist, accredited coach, supervisor and director of the Henley Centre for Coaching, Henley Business School.

Vicious Flower

Ingredients

Pen

Paper

Description

This technique has its origins in Cognitive Behavioural Therapy. It follows the shape of a flower – hence its name. The centre states a problem, which is around a belief that is causing a problem, and the petals state various maintenance processes. Maintenance processes are defined as psychological processes that keep the problem going. It is a cycle where the initial thoughts give rise to behaviours that as a result confirm the initial belief and prolong the problem. For example, "I believe I am a bad presenter, so before a presentation I get anxious and start shaking, I struggle to concentrate, and as a consequence I present badly, and this 'confirms' that I must be a bad presenter." As a result of the belief and maintaining thoughts, this unhelpful belief continues. This technique divides the problem into workable parts. Each maintenance process is looked at individually and the person can visualise the impact and work on them one by one to make it more manageable.

Common maintenance processes include:
- Escape/avoidance – because the client avoids the situation, they do not learn coping strategies and/or they don't allow disconfirmation;
- Reduction of activity – because the client withdraws (an activity is seen as unenjoyable or as too demanding), they don't get positive rewards such as pleasure, achievement, acceptance;
- Hypervigilance – because the client is constantly checking, they notice things that they would not otherwise do, and interpret them to be confirmatory;
- Performance anxiety – because the client feels anxious, their performance is affected negatively, and they blame the belief rather than the anxiety;
- Seeking short-term rewards – because they allow short-term rewards, they have long-term consequences (Kennerley, 2016).

Step by step

1. Together with the client, name the problem they are experiencing and identify the thought/belief behind that problem.
2. After exploring this, draw a circle and place the belief in the centre.
3. Explain to the client that, together as a team, you are now going to explore the processes that may be getting in their way, in order to stop this problem.
4. Ask them first if they have any hypothesis themselves. If not, help them to think about it by asking about:
   a. Emotions that may be showing up such as fear and anxiety

Vicious Flower

b. Behaviours such as avoidance, escape (hiding one's true self), reduction of activity or overcompensation behaviours

a. Self-fulfilling prophecies (where the client changes their behaviour to a maintenance behaviour, causing people around them to react differently, which is then in turn taken as confirmation)

c. Seeking reassurance

d. Hypervigilance (where the person notices normal behaviours that would otherwise be overlooked and takes them as proof of their belief)

e. Catastrophic misinterpretation (where the person feels the symptoms of anxiety and interprets them as a verification of a problem, in turn increasing the symptoms), and

f. Perfectionism.

First write the output and then how it might be feeding the problem (the effect of).

Reference

Kennerley, H. (2016) *An Introduction to Cognitive Behaviour Therapy: Skills and Applications* (3rd edition). Thousand Oaks, CA: SAGE Publications Ltd.

Claudia Day is an accredited coach and entrepreneur with a marketing strategy background and trained in coaching at Henley Business School and management at MIT Sloan.

5. Think of ways in which each petal could be challenged to change the dynamic and, together with the client, build possible tests.

Coaching through Transitions (Bridges' Transition Model)

Ingredients

Optional – image of transition model

Pen and paper

When does it work best?

The model works best for individuals experiencing transition, whether it is on the horizon, is occurring now or has recently happened. It can be especially helpful for externally imposed transition (e.g. involuntary redundancy) where there is a particular feeling of lack of control. It is also relevant for those making a transition by choice (e.g. returning to work from parental leave) where there is a recognition that there will be an inevitable shift in daily life and working norms.

Description

Bridges' transition model (Bridges, 1991) offers a framework to understand and navigate the psychological and practical impact of transitions. Originally used to explain organisational change, it is equally practical for use in individual coaching thanks to its visual and simple nature. Transitions are typified by three key phases – endings, the neutral zone and new beginnings. The model's underlying premise is that individuals should be encouraged to be wholly involved throughout the process of transition to counteract feelings of lack of control. The model suggests that each transition phase has distinct emotional characteristics experienced by the individual. The coach encourages the client to become more aware of their feelings at each phase through powerful questions. (The framework can also be overlaid with the Kubler-Ross change cycle – Kubler-Ross, 1969.) The coach then supports the client to develop practical strategies to counter the negative emotions and improve their belief that they are 'in the driving seat' of the present and future. Being able to make sense of transitions over time and creating elements of control has an immensely positive impact on wellbeing.

Step by step

1. Introduce the framework and explain that it is intended to help the client to navigate change and provide them with greater control over their situation.
2. Recognise the endings phase, when a change has occurred, by celebrating the achievements of the past. Ask the individual to diagnose what will change and what will stay the same. What will they be leaving behind, how will their status change, who will have responsibility for decision-making now? Encourage self-awareness of personal feelings. (Common feelings at this stage include shock, sadness, anger, confusion and denial.) Consider practical rituals to mark this phase.
3. Reframe the neutral zone phase, when the old is gone but the new isn't fully operational. Encourage self-awareness of personal feelings. (Common feelings at this stage include ambiguity, disorientation, apathy, confusion and lethargy.) Consider practical strategies to reframe the situation as an opportunity for learning, creativity and planning for a more positive future.

Coaching through Transitions (Bridges' Transition Model)

4. Create the beginnings phase, when new attitudes and behaviours are developed. Encourage self-awareness of personal feelings. (Common feelings at this stage include acceptance, positive energy, excitement, openness and relief.) Consider practical strategies to move forward with a job search, return planning or skills development. Examples include: gathering information, narrative building, accounting for gaps, networking and acquiring new technical qualifications.

5. Acknowledge that transition is a process. It is not always linear and the boundaries between phases can often be blurred, but each phase *will* pass!

Reference

Bridges, W. (1991) *Managing Transitions: Making the Most of Change.* Cambridge, MA: Da Capo Press.

Kubler-Ross, E. (1969) *On Death and Dying.* Macmillan, New York.

Pippa Ruxton is an accredited executive coach providing rigorous, tailored and practical coaching, supported by extensive coaching experience and a successful international corporate career.

Water Tank

Ingredients

A piece of paper and a pen

When does it work best?

It can be used with individuals and whole teams that need to increase their awareness of their own wellbeing or energy levels to perform at their best. Becoming more mindful of your own level, how you top it up and what drains it, puts you in control. You can also support others if you create a common, sometimes playful language around the water tank that allows people to genuinely share how they are doing and if they need some help.

Mike Phillips brings over 30 years of international business experience to his coaching practice helping people ride the waves of change.

Description

There are times when it is particularly important for leaders and their leadership teams to look after themselves, as well as their people. The water tank is a metaphor for looking at your own energy levels, mindful that to perform at your best you need the energy to do so and that there are things you can do to fill it up and things that will drain it.

The tool also offers the opportunity to create a new shared common language in teams that allows members to check in with each other in an abstract way. "How full is your tank?" or "what level are you at?" is ok to ask and answer genuinely, whereas asking "how are you?" in the UK or US will almost always get the answer "I'm fine".

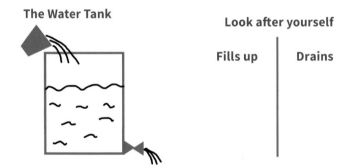

The Water Tank

How well have your strategies been working to ensure there is enough water in your tank

Look after yourself

Fills up | **Drains**

Activity – Make a list of what tops up and drains your tank, then discuss...

Step by step

1. Sketch a water tank (on the left side of an A4 page in landscape) then:
   a. Add a level of water (around half full)
   b. Add an input valve or bucket (to fill it up)
   c. Add a drain valve (from which it empties).
2. Explain the metaphor to the client: the tank represents the client, and the water level represent their energy level at a moment in time (their thinking, feeling, doing energies; or they could think of the level as their wellbeing).
3. Check with the client that they understand the metaphor.
4. On the right side of the page, draw a vertical line to split the page in two and then write the headings 'Fill up' and 'Drain' on either side of the line.
5. Invite the client to list and discuss what fills the tank (e.g. sleep, exercise, the right food).
6. Invite the client to list and discuss what drains the tank (e.g. the boss's behaviour, multiple project deadlines in the same week).

Water Tank

7. Invite the client to reflect on the message: "To be in the best shape to get things done, be mindful about doing those things that fill your tank before you start."
8. When using the metaphor with a team, seek permission to ask each other "how full is your water tank?" and help each other to fill them up.

Lego Build: Building Wellbeing

Ingredients

Lego (any amount or type)

When does it work best?

This Lego build works best as a starting point in coaching when the client knows that something needs their attention but is unsure of what it is. It helps them explore their wellbeing and focus on what might not be serving them well at this moment in time.

Description

Wellbeing is buildable. It isn't just the absence of negative functions such as depression, loneliness and illness, but the presence of positive attributes (such as happiness, connection and wellness) that make a person's life fulfilling. Wellbeing can be explored using the five pillars of PERMA:

- **P** – Positive emotions
- **E** – Engagement
- **R** – Relationships
- **M** – Meaning
- **A** – Accomplishment.

When we pay deliberate attention to these interrelated areas of wellbeing and take positive action towards them, we have the potential to improve individual, organisational and community wellbeing. Building Lego models in coaching provides a coaching environment of psychological safety that allows the client time to think, enabling the creation of new awareness, insights and a greater self-efficacy. Following the Triple-E approach to coaching – *Engage*, *Explore* and *Expand* – the client becomes comfortable building models in Lego and using the model to explore insights, which can be expanded and applied to their life. This task invites your client to explore their own wellbeing and, if necessary, focus on the one element that is not aligned in more depth.

Step by step

Prior to the session, ensure that you are familiar with using Lego and have tried the build questions.

1. Frame the building opportunity with your client to ensure that it is a relevant question for them.
2. **Engage** the client with the warm up task: *"Using the bricks in front of you, build a tower-like construction. Build the highest tower possible, making sure it can stand on its own. You have three minutes."*
3. Share the building question: what makes them feel good? *"Your task is to build a model that enables you to share a story of what makes you feel good. You have 20 minutes."*
4. Allow the client the time and space to **explore** the build silently, whilst being there to answer any questions they may have.
5. Once the model is complete, invite your client to share their story.
6. Use the following coaching questions to **explore** the model further.

Coaching questions:

P: What emotions come up for you when you view your model? That emotion looks like what?

E: What elements of your model fire you up? What does it look like when you use what makes you sparkle to be more engaged?

Lego Build: Building Wellbeing

R: What needs to happen with your connections? What one small step could you make today to move closer to the connection you need?

M: Where in your model are you fulfilled? How can you incorporate that to bring purpose and meaning to other areas in your life?

A: What in your model enables you to meet challenges and set goals? How can you use this strength to help you achieve?

7. **Expand** by investigating new insights more deeply and continuing the coaching conversation or by identifying follow-up actions and new potential behaviours.

Theresa Quinn is a coaching psychologist and positive psychologist who is building thought change one brick at a time.

Accountability Loop

Ingredients

Accountability loop diagram

Description

This accountability model (Samuel, 2012) is designed to present a choice of different responses to a situation: either to recognise it or to ignore it. Recognition drives ownership that, ultimately, leads to forgiveness, growth and positive action to resolve the situation. In other words, taking accountability. On the other hand, being a victim usually begins by choosing to ignore the root cause of a situation. This leads to denial, blame and post-rationalisation of the situation. Ultimately, positive action is resisted and, rather than learning from the situation, one hides from it.

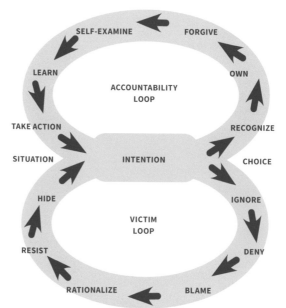

Step by step

1. A client describes a situation and a dilemma as to what to do.
2. Introduce the diagram to the client.
3. The coach uses the loops of the diagram, initially following the victim loop, helping the client consider how they might choose to respond in a situation when following the first loop.
4. The coach then invites the client to consider the second loop: what actions would follow if the client chose to be accountable for their situation?
5. Having followed both loops, the client is in a better position to make a choice as to which loop is appropriate in the situation.

Reference

Samuel, M. (2012) *Making Yourself Indispensable: The Power of Personal Accountability*. Portfolio.

Aidan Kerr has 23 years of leadership experience and is a Henley executive coach.

Lurodivye – The Holy Fool

Ingredients

None

When does it work best?

The technique works best when a client cannot see their own hubris, and those around them feign or follow what they say. This lack of self-awareness happens to leaders (Owen, 2018) and is a difficult challenge for them to overcome. The coach can be in a unique position to share a different perspective and to name things as they see it. But be careful: no-one likes to be made to be considered to be naked, and it is sometimes the messenger who takes the bullet.

Jonathan Passmore is a chartered psychologist, accredited coach, supervisor and director of the Henley Centre for Coaching, Henley Business School.

Description

In the Eastern Orthodox Christian faith, there is an archetype known as the *Lurodivye* or the Holy Fool. This character is a social misfit, marked by subversive behaviour, who feigns a type of madness in order to provide the public with 'spiritual guidance' while avoiding praise for their saintly behaviour. The character often talks in riddles, but nonetheless has access to the truth. The Holy Fool is a truth teller, not in spite of being, but because he is an outcast. He does not worry about social conventions, norms or popularity. He says it like it is. We can see variations of this character in many popular stories. One example is in Hans Christian Anderson's tale 'The Emperor's New Clothes'. In the story, the Emperor commissions fancy new clothes from two swindlers, who tell everyone that the cloth is so fine, only intelligent people can see it, thus implying that only fools will see nothing. Everyone is too scared of their social status to say what they really see, and it takes a child to point out that the Emperor is naked. Only a child can do this, as the boy was not thinking about his social status but simply spoke the truth as he saw it. The closest we have to a Holy Fool in modern organisations are whistle-blowers and executive coaches.

Step by step

1. Contract with clients at the start around both confidentiality and challenge. Making clear you are on the client's side, while your role is to bring challenge that others do not see or say, due to their compromised position. Remind the client that, while you are friendly, you are not their friend, but what you do is in service of them and their longer-term development agenda.
2. When you identify an issue, try to gather data from multiple perspectives.
3. Invite the client to reflect on their perspective and how others might see it.
4. Invite the client to consider 'enemy' perspectives.
5. In this way, you have moved them to recognise there is more than one way to see the issue, even if the client does not see it as you do.
6. Check back to the contract in terms of challenge and, with the client's agreement, deliver the perspective.
7. Invite the client not to respond, but to consider what if some people saw it this way, how might this potentially impact on them? What risks would this bring? How might they seek to manage the issue?
8. In future sessions return to the theme, if it is a critical issue, to encourage the client to consider this as a legitimate perspective and thus one that needs to be taken into account. Even if it is not accepted as 'the truth' – it may be a truth for some and thus do damage.

Secret Admirer (Strength Spotting)

Ingredients

A VIA Character Strengths Assessment (www.viacharacter.org)

One pack of Character Strengths cards (optional – https://www.thepositivityinstitute.com.au/product/character-strength-cards)

Attitude: a good dose of mindfulness and compassion

Description

Humans have a negativity bias (Rozin and Royzman, 2001); that is, we're wired to look for things that can go wrong and/or harm us. This bias is there to protect us and does a very good job of that at the times it's needed. We've also been socialised to focus on what's not working well for us at school and at work, and we're told to work hard at rectifying or developing these weaknesses. In addition, many people experience stronger negativity biases than others, perhaps having grown up in a family or with a parent who held a very strong pessimistic bias, whereby there was a scanning and focused attention on all of the bad things in people and the world. We also know that "bad is stronger than good" (Baumeister et al., 2001), meaning that bad emotions, bad parents and bad feedback have more impact than good ones, and bad information is processed more thoroughly than good. Overall, this means we have to work extra hard at focusing on what's working well and in finding all of the good in ourselves, others and the world. One way of doing this is to bring our mindful attention to someone we love to consciously and compassionately identify their character strengths – that is, their innate positive traits such as kindness, leadership or hope. There are 24 character strengths that are universal and morally valued, and you can read more about them at the VIA Institute website (www.viacharacter.org).

When does it work best?

The exercise is helpful in the following situations:
1. When a client is first learning about character strengths, to help build character strengths literacy and an increased awareness of strengths in self and others;
2. When a client has a challenging relationship with someone and there is a desire to improve that relationship;
3. When a client is a leader and wants to improve their team's relationships and effectiveness.

Step by step

1. Introduce the client to the research behind the negativity bias, 'bad is stronger than good' and the negative impact this can potentially have (e.g. depression, relationship difficulties).
2. Highlight the research on the power of learning to consciously focus on the good in ourselves, others and the world through gratitude, savouring and strength-spotting.

Secret Admirer (Strength Spotting)

3. Introduce the concept of character strengths and provide a brief rationale as to the benefits of strengths knowledge, use and spotting. Ask the client to complete the VIA Character Strengths Assessment (www.viacharacter.org) to familiarise themselves with the 24 character strengths.
4. Ask the client to identify someone who they would like to start viewing differently, from a strengths perspective.
5. If the client is undertaking the exercise with their team, ask them to write everyone's name on small pieces of paper and place them into a hat (or other type of container). Then ask each person to draw a name out of the hat and not share with anyone the name of the person whom they have drawn.
6. Ask the client to practise 'strength-spotting' (secretly admiring, if you like ;-) that person over a period of time, say 2–3 months. Use the VIA as a reference and look for strengths in the person.
7. After a period of time, ask the client to write a description of what they have observed. Ask them to provide concrete examples of where they've seen strengths in action. Ask the client to reflect on what they've seen and how they might be viewing that person differently now. Suggest they might type it up to give to the person at a future date.
8. If in a team, set a date for a team meeting where each person will announce who they were 'secretly admiring'. One person starts and announces their 'spottee' and then that person announces their spottee, until everyone has had a turn.

References

Baumeister, R.F., Bratslavsky, E., Finkenauer, C., and Vohs, K.D. (2001) Bad is Stronger than Good. *Review of General Psychology*, 5(4), 323–70.

Rozin, P., and Royzman, E. (2001) Negativity Bias, Negativity Dominance, and Contagion. *Personality and Social Psychology Review*, 5, 296–320.

Suzy Green is a clinical and coaching psychologist, the founder of the Positivity Institute and has published on the integration of positive psychology and coaching psychology over the past 20 years.

Leaves on a Stream

Ingredients

None

If outdoors – two or three leaves

When does it work best?

The technique works best for clients within an ACT framework, where the client is struggling to manage unhelpful, negative or illogical thinking. Rather than encourage the client to dispute the thinking through a more evidenced-based perspective, ACT encourages the client to recognise that these thoughts are not the truth, they are not part of who they are as a person: the client has the choice to ignore these thoughts and to move on to more productive thinking.

Description

This technique is based on Acceptance and Commitment coaching and, like many ACT techniques, uses a metaphor to help the client to reframe their thinking about a problem or issue (Harris, 2009). The technique aims to help clients to recognise that their thoughts are separate from them, and that these thoughts are transitory: today's thoughts will be different to next week's, and different again next month or next year. The technique involves inviting the client to place their negative or unhelpful thoughts on an imaginary (or real) leaf and to imagine (or watch) the leaf, and their thought, float away. For some clients, it can be helpful to explain the metaphor and for them to include this as a technique they start to use themselves when unhelpful or negative thoughts invade their mind.

Step by step

1. The client may express their unhelpful thought: *"I can't help thinking they will find out I am an imposter and am not up to the job."*
2. Invite the client to reframe these thoughts. *"I have found some clients have discovered that it is useful to recognise these thoughts are simply just that – thoughts. They are not truer than any other thought you have or could have. One way to do this is to imagine placing the thought on a leaf and then watching it float away down a gentle stream. Can I invite you to bring the thought to mind? Now imagine placing the thought on a leaf and watching as it gently glides away from you. If you are aware of other thoughts coming to mind, place them on a leaf too, and repeat the process."*
3. The coach holds the silence in this process for 20 or 30 seconds, and may follow with a question: *"How does that feel?"*
4. The coach may ask: *"How might you use this technique when other unhelpful thoughts come to mind?"*

Reference

Harris, R. (2009) *ACT Made Simple*. Oakland, CA: New Harbinger Publications, Inc.

Kaveh Mir is an MCC ICF coach and tutor on the Henley coaching programmes.

Vision Board

Ingredients

Table surface or large sheet of paper

Pens

Post-it notes

Coaching cards with pictures, or magazines and scissors

Phone/camera

Description

The development of a vision board with a client allows them to be creative when exploring their goal/s and/or future pathways they may be looking to embark on. The completed vision board allows a client to have a snapshot (or 'one pager') of what this will look like, which they can display or refer to as a prompt and reminder. It also allows a client to track their progress.

Step by step

1. Spread coaching cards or magazines out for the client to review on the table.
2. Invite the client to choose one image that represents the end goal (or one image for each goal set). Place this on a large surface or sheet of paper.
3. Discuss with the client what actions or steps they are going to take to reach that goal/s. (It can be useful to ask the client to stand and take a few steps back from the image, to get a broader perspective on their goal/s. Ask them to take a step forward once they have identified the first step or action they would take, asking them to explain that step or action through.)
4. Invite the client to choose images that may represent these steps or actions.
5. Invite the client to place these images (in whichever way they want) on the surface or large sheet of paper.
6. Prompt the client to write any words (on Post-it notes) that they may wish to add to the vision board, to reinforce any meaning on why or what this action is about.
7. Once the board is complete, ensure that a photo is taken of the vision board, which can then be printed out or digitally kept in a place where a client can view it regularly.
8. It can be useful for a client to then share this vision board with someone who they believe can support them, via informal check-ins.

When does it work best?

Working with a vision board works well with clients who are creative, and those that prefer a more visual approach. It also works well when people have set or established longer-term goals and/or there are several pathways to achieving these. It works well when working with teams too, for example, teams embarking on a new journey or project.

Deb McEwen is an experienced accredited coach who has held senior leadership roles (NZ, AU and UK) and has an extensive background in health and wellbeing.

What Do I Really Want?

Ingredients

Pen and paper

When does it work best?

The technique works best when a client is at a transition or decision point about the future and unsure about which way to go. They may be feeling stuck and wanting to make changes. The technique can be set as a homework task, to be discussed at the next coaching session.

Description

This is a reflective exercise that involves journaling responses to the question: "What do I really want?" It can help clients get in touch with what really matters to them, enabling them to connect with their energy for change and options for a way forward. It allows for possibilities, desires and dreams to emerge and also touches on gratitude by identifying what is already there for them in their lives. Some clients have never really addressed this question. It can also give them permission to start to replace 'should' with 'want to'. The power of using expressive writing enables a different sort of focus and listening to the answers that emerge. It helps the client to generate greater clarity and congruence to what can be a difficult question for them. It can also help to increase gratitude and lead to a deeper appreciation about who they really are, their identity and what they really want.

Step by step

1. As a homework task, the coach invites the client to undertake writing an answer to the question: "What do I really want?" The coach will encourage the client to use four different lenses by asking the question four times and, each time, putting the emphasis on the next element of the question: "What – do I – really – want?" The coach invites the client to journal their responses for up to five minutes between each question.
2. The coach should explain the different emphasis for each question.
    *   '**What**' – materially, the goals, achievements, relationships, work and the tangible things that they want in life.
    *   'Do **I**' – not anybody else (parents, friends, partners, colleagues). What do *they themself* want? How can they be more fully themself? How would they be different if they were really shining?
    *   '**Really**' – so much so that they would be willing to take risks for it. Truly. Heartfelt. This could include relationships, impact on others, work, vocation. What do they really want to do/say?
    *   '**Want**' – their deepest desire, or maybe in the sense of "is there anything I lack?" It's also a reminder of gratitude, of what they have already.
3. At the next session, invite the client to reflect on the process and the outcomes: What did they noticed about their energy when they considered their different responses to the questions? What emerged? What do they now want to go and do?

Jacqui Zanetti is an executive coach with a corporate background and a strong interest in international leadership.

The Dynamic Careers Coaching Model

Ingredients

Paper and pen

Attitude of mind:
reflective

When does it work best?

At its core, this
model aims to help
clients enhance
skill-building
during periods of
high uncertainty
and develop the
skillsets that will
be needed in a
more automated
world. Such skills
include adopting a
hyper-flexible,
people- and
results-focused
approach.
Fundamentally, it
is about knowing
how to survive and
thrive in the face of
automation, using
a three-stage
process.

Description

The critical element to thriving (and surviving) at work is knowing how to be dynamic, especially when faced with huge external changes. We've seen around us the impact of a global pandemic – but also the impact of digital technology on the world of work. Both have created enormous uncertainty and ambiguity. During the pandemic, organisations made step changes in how to work while not being 'at work'. But there is more to technology than communications and automation. How will we cope when the robots come (or rather, once they are here in droves)? We need a career-planning model that can help clients manage high levels of uncertainty.

Step by step

1. *First*, we need to be **results** orientated – to be proactive, to set goals, have a clear focus and constantly monitor the changing world of work.
   a. How is the environment changing?
   b. What are the 'essentials' of this environment?
   c. How regularly do you review your goals?
   d. What are the blocks in your way?
2. This is tempered by the *second* part – the need to be **resourceful** when acting on new data.
   a. How do you monitor the external climate – your sensemaking skills?
   b. How do you adapt your goals?
   c. When do you enhance your pursuit of your goal, when do you let it go?
   d. How do you stay 'self-reliant'?
3. And finally, the *third* step: it is essential to have a strong **relationship** focus in order to drive the people-engagement processes.
   a. Who is your 'personal board of directors' and how do you make best use of these individuals (as well as pay back)?
   b. How can you build your network? What do you do to offer to others in your network?
   c. How are you building your emotional intelligence?

Naeema Pasha currently
leads on Careers,
Professional
Development and Future
of Work at Henley
Business School.

Becoming BOXER

Ingredients

Book: *Animal Farm* (optional)

When does it work best?

The tool works well when the client feels they are spending all their time at work, working their hardest but getting nowhere even when they desperately want a promised utopia. They believe their loyalty will automatically be seen and rewarded. You can approach this either as a coach or as a mentor.

Reference

Orwell, G. (2000) *Animal Farm*. London: Penguin.

Jonathan Drew is a former British ambassador and high commissioner, and is currently Vice President of the ICF UK Chapter and a fellow of the Royal College of Physicians of Edinburgh.

Description

Many people will be familiar with George Orwell's seminal work, *Animal Farm*. The story is about a group of animals that start a revolt against their human masters and win their independence. As time moves on, gradually the pigs begin to dominate the rest of the animals, becoming more and more like humans, until they are indistinguishable from them. The book serves as an allegory for the Russian Revolution.

Within the story there is a loyal, trusting horse – Boxer – who always agrees to do anything that is asked of him because he believes that any problem can be solved if he works harder and because he believes that by working harder, he will reach the utopia that the pigs promise and in which he believes. In the end, in accepting anything that is thrown at him, he injures himself. The pigs, seeing an opportunity, say he's being sent into retirement, but he's actually carted off to the knacker's yard and killed for horsemeat.

This tale within a tale warns against both overworking and blind loyalty. Too often, clients think that these things will help them reach their objectives, but this is rarely the case. Instead, the client may get further and produce far better results for their organisation through better use of their time and more differentiation between their workstreams.

Step by step

1. Ask the client if they have read *Animal Farm* and recall the horse Boxer.
2. Remind them of the key details.
3. Challenge them around your observation that there are similarities between what you are hearing from them and Boxer.
4. Ask them to reflect on the following coach's calibrated questions that might help them become a different 'BOXER':
   - What is the **B**alance in your work life (between your different pieces of work)?
   - When do you feel you are **O**verdoing it?
   - What's your own **X**anadu for which you are striving at work?
   - What causes an **E**ager response in you – and how often do you *Express it*?
   - How often do you pay attention to your **R**esilience?
5. Explain to them that the first letters of the key words from each vital ingredient spell 'BOXER' – a better Boxer than the one in *Animal Farm*.

Mindful HERO

Ingredients

Pen and paper

Optional: Positive Transformation Cards (Boniwell, 2018)

Description

Research has discovered four specific psychological characteristics (hope, confidence, resilience and optimism) that increase our ability to handle problems efficiently and enable us to project ourselves effectively into the future. The HERO model encompasses these four characteristics and has been defined as psychological capital, an individual's positive psychological state of functioning that is characterised by: (1) persevering toward goals and, when necessary, adjusting paths towards those goals in order to succeed (**H**ope); (2) having the confidence to take on challenging tasks and putting in the necessary effort to succeed (**E**fficacy); (3) when faced with problems and adversity, overcoming them and bouncing back, and even beyond, (**R**esilience) to achieve success; (4) making positive attributions (**O**ptimism) about succeeding now and in the future.

Research has demonstrated that an individual who possesses high levels of all four of these characteristics also consistently performs at a higher level (Luthans et al., 2007). Recently, a fifth element has been proposed as part of the model and the starting point of the HERO journey: Mindfulness, the ability to intentionally pay full attention to the present moment (Luthans, Youssef and Avolio, 2015). A Mindful HERO is thus someone who is able to be fully present in their current reality in order to take a step forward with no fear of failure.

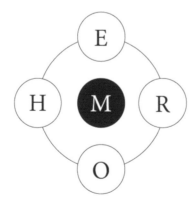

Mindful HERO

Step by step

1. Ask your client to select a challenging situation or a transformation goal that they would like to work on.
2. Use the Question Cards (or questions below) and follow the Mindful HERO model to create a spread of five cards.
3. Encourage your client to choose these cards deliberately, one from each of the categories, allowing themselves to be drawn in by an image. Lay them out in a circle with the Mindful card in the centre.
4. Questions:

   Mindful – This is the card that represents your actual position or situation. What do you see in this photo? What is it telling you? What is the change that needs to happen? What are you not noticing?

   Hope – What do you hope for? What is your goal? Where would you like to go? How can you get there? How else can you get there? What will motivate you to start?

   Efficacy – How do you feel about this journey? Look at the colours, shapes and details emerging from the picture: what do these tell you about yourself? How confident do you feel about the challenge awaiting you?

   Resilience – What are the difficulties you are likely to encounter along the way? How can you best prepare for these obstacles? What resources do you have that would help you overcome them?

   Optimism – What do you need to do, or believe, to ensure that the result is positive? Are you now ready to step into the unknown? What will be your first step?

5. Having completed the process, ask your client to turn the cards over and read the quotes. How can their insights and resolutions be enhanced by the thoughts of the wise?

References

Boniwell, I. (2018) *Positive Transformation Cards: The Mindful HERO Journey.* Paris: Positran.

Luthans, F., Avolio, B.J., Avey, J.B., and Norman, S.M. (2007) Positive Psychological Capital: Measurement and Relationship with Performance and Satisfaction. *Personnel Psychology*, 60(3), 541–72.

Luthans, F., Youssef, C.M., and Avolio, B.J. (2015) *Psychological Capital and Beyond.* Oxford University Press, USA.

Ilona Boniwell is a renowned positive psychologist, a tutor at Henley Centre for Coaching, programme director at Anglia Ruskin and CEO of Positran.

Lego Build: When I'm Working at My Best

Ingredients

Lego (any amount or type)

When does it work best?

The narrative approach of using Lego works best when a client is looking to explore thinking in greater depth. This particularly works well for exploring ideas that have already arisen in coaching, to open up new awareness and to use learning to make changes and adapt practices. It allows a tangible under-standing and clarity for moving forward. As one client said: "It actually clarifies in your own mind what you're thinking, because you can have a thought but then to represent it visually, you have to understand what it means."

Description

Building Lego models in coaching provides a coaching environment of psycho-logical safety that allows the client time to think, enabling the creation of new awareness, insights and a greater self-efficacy. Following the Triple-E approach to coaching – *Engage*, *Explore* and *Expand* – the client becomes comfortable building models in Lego and uses the model to explore insights that can be expanded and applied to the client's life. Following a Lego warm up that famil-iarises the client with Lego and helps to create a flow, they are invited to explore the Lego build question: *"Your task is to build a model that enables you to answer the question: when I am working at my best, it's like what?"* As the client builds, the process switches between reflecting on the question and constructing the model, developing the hand–mind connection. The client's hands feed the mind, opening up a world of possibilities, which allows the creation of tangible representations of thoughts. Once built, the story and symbols the model holds are shared and become the basis for the coaching conversation that follows, either adding further layers of understanding to the build or identifying potential actions and new behaviours.

Step by step

Prior to the session, ensure that you are familiar with using Lego and have tried the build question.

1. Frame the building opportunity with your client to ensure that it is a relevant question for them.
2. **Engage** the client with the warm-up task: *"Using the bricks in front of you, build a tower-like construction. Build the highest tower possible, making sure it can stand on its own. You have three minutes."*
3. Share the building question: *"Your task is to build a model that enables you to answer the question: 'when I am working at my best, it's like what?' You have 20 minutes. 'Work' can mean anything you do."*
4. Allow the client the time and space to **explore** the build silently, whilst being there to answer any questions they may have.
5. Once the model is complete, invite your client to share their story.
6. Use your coaching questions and skills to **explore** the model further. The model shouldn't be challenged, so use questions to allow the client to consider different ideas, opportunities and perspectives; explore their strengths, what lights them up.
7. **Expand** by investigating new insights more deeply and continuing the coaching conversation or by identifying follow-up actions and new potential behaviours.

Theresa Quinn is a coaching psychologist and positive psychologist who is building thought change one brick at a time.

A Little Bit of H-O-P-E

Ingredients

None

When does it work best?

It works best when the coach feels that their client is displaying low levels of confidence. The coach may observe this low confidence, hope or enthusiasm through the client's language, tone of voice and statements. After exploring with the client, the coach might encourage the client to quickly take some easy-to-handle tasks so that the client regains confidence and enhanced enthusiasm for their plan.

Reference

Bandura, A. (1997) *Self-efficacy: The Exercise of Control*. New York: Freeman.

Badri Bajaj is a leading coach and researcher, and imparts coaching training to individuals and organisations.

Description

H-O-P-E is different from hope. H-O-P-E is an acronym for Hurry, Opportunity, Positivity and Enthusiasm. Sometimes clients don't hold hope about achieving their goals due to their negative attitudes, past experiences, unsupportive environment, lack of resources, work stress and many other factors. In these circumstances, the coach needs to raise the confidence of their clients by engaging them in easy steps to achieve goals. These success experiences raise confidence levels in the client and increase their hope. The coach invites their clients to take baby steps, which can ultimately lead to mastery (Bandura, 1997). In undertaking this process, the coach needs to help clients plan simple baby steps, quickly, so that they can maintain momentum in the coaching journey. Coaches also need to support their clients to develop a positive attitude towards themselves, their goals and their environments.

Step by step

1. Ask the client to share one or more very small actions, which they think might move them one step towards their goal.
2. The coach may also engage the client to visualise the execution of these small tasks.
3. The coach may check how the client would know if this small step had been achieved, and when they plan to take it.
4. In follow-up conversations, further small steps can be planned and made, which move the client one step at a time towards their goal and, through this, gradually build self-efficacy on the journey.

True Self

Ingredients

A private space to write

Pen and paper

When does it work best?

The exercise works best in coaching contexts where the client may be lacking confidence in their ability to fulfil a prosocial goal or role; that is, behaving in a way that helps to protect the welfare, rights and feelings of other people. They may be feeling disappointed by their own lack of awareness, past mistakes or action; this is sometimes linked to attitudes or behaviours that have resided outside of their conscious awareness (for example, unconscious bias).

Description

The theory of the true self posits that at our core, all human beings are naturally inclined towards morally virtuous behaviour. We tend to believe that we are all inherently good and noble, deep down inside. Whether or not the theory of the true self is indeed 'true' (Strohminger, Knobe and Newman, 2017), thinking about a true self has been shown to increase prosocial behaviour and reduce intergroup bias (De Freitas and Cikara, 2018). On first glance, the True Self activity may appear quite similar to the Best Possible Self activity (King, 2001); however, an important distinction is that a *possible* self is described as a personal manifestation of goals (Markus and Nurius, 1986) whereas the *true* self aligns with inherent personal attributes that we believe already exist within us. The theory of the true self allows people to identify their core strengths and virtues, and to perceive this as an achievable benchmark against which to compare their current behaviour. The True Self exercise, combined with strengths or positive psychology coaching, can be used to enhance self-awareness and a belief in one's own abilities to behave virtuously, and to engage in self-concordant goal setting (Moin and van Nieuwerburgh, 2021).

Step by step

1. Invite the client to take part in a self-reflective written exercise lasting 10–15 minutes.
2. Ensure that they are in a private space where they can write freely without the concern of anyone else reading what they have written (this includes you, the coach, so the exercise may be best utilised as in-between-sessions work).
3. Remind them that they need not be concerned about spelling or grammatical accuracy. Then provide them with the following instructions:
   Imagine you are in a context where you are meeting and interacting with a broad range of people. Imagine there are people from all walks of life, both familiar and unfamiliar. There is the opportunity to approach all individuals equally. Now imagine you are your true best self in this situation. Who are you? How do you behave? How do you feel? What do you do? How do you contribute to your social interactions and relationships? What role do you play in a group, society or community? Establish a clear vision of your true best self by writing for the next 10–15 minutes.
4. When you next meet with the client, as the coach, explore the client's response to this exercise and ask questions to support them in assimilating their vision of a true self with their actual self.

True Self

5. Applying a strengths coaching approach, it is helpful to ask the client to consider which strengths and virtues they demonstrated in their vision of their true self, past examples of when they have been their true self and how they feel about their true self, identifying unrealised strengths and exploring potential for further development.
6. Positive psychology coaching prioritises wellbeing as well as performance; therefore, it is also helpful to explore how behaving in a manner consistent with the true self influences the client's wellbeing and the quality of their relationships, as well as the wellbeing of those with whom they interact.
7. Leverage the insights from this exercise to support the client in creating prosocial intentions and commitments that are aligned with their motivations and strengths.

References

De Freitas, J., and Cikara, M. (2018) Deep Down My Enemy Is Good: Thinking about the True Self Reduces Intergroup Bias. *Journal of Experimental Social Psychology*, 74, 307–16. https://doi.org/10.1016/j.jesp.2017.10.006

King, L.A. (2001) The Health Benefits of Writing about Life Goals. *Personality and Social Psychology Bulletin*, 27(7), 798–807. https://doi.org/10.1177/0146167201277003

Markus, H., and Nurius, P. (1986) Possible Selves. *American Psychologist*, 41(9), 954–69. https://doi.org/10.1037/0003-066X.41.9.954

Moin, F.K.T., and van Nieuwerburgh, C. (2021) The Experience of Positive Psychology Coaching Following Unconscious Bias Training: An Interpretative Phenomenological Analysis. *International Journal of Evidence-based Coaching and Mentoring*.

Strohminger, N., Knobe, J., and Newman, G. (2017) The True Self: A Psychological Concept Distinct from the Self. *Perspectives on Psychological Science*, 12(4), 551–60.

Tia Moin is an organisational and coaching psychologist, academic supervisor and coaching researcher who specialises in positive psychology coaching for inclusion.

Hedges and Potholes – Team Coaching

Ingredients

None

Description

Hedges and potholes offer two metaphors to consider the risks that can occur on projects. In this case, the hedges are clearly observed risks, which are known and can be planned for; potholes are unforeseen risks, which if not planned for, can derail the project.

Step by step

1. Describe the model to the client: Hedges and Potholes.
2. Encourage the client (or team) to list the hedges that have been identified.
3. Explore with the client (or team) actions planned to overcome these hedges.
4. Repeat the process for the potholes.
5. Challenge more strongly around potential potholes and around project management to reduce the risks of unforeseen potholes derailing the project, using techniques such as the 13th Fairy to explore hidden stakeholders.

When does it work best?

This technique works well in team or individual coaching when exploring a period of change or on a new project. It helps the individual or team to reflect more deeply on risk and plan for both foreseen and unforeseen events, while also putting in place project management to monitor for hidden potholes.

Adeola Oludemi is a Henley-trained leadership coach, curious about the data concealed within emotion and how it influences our behaviours.

If You Were a Tree

Ingredients

Nine pictures of different kinds of trees in different surroundings

Or real trees, if walking outside

Description

'If You Were a Tree', with supporting images, is a Finnish technique and can help the client to think more broadly, not using only their 'head', but linking their 'heart' and their 'gut'. The client may react in different ways, focusing on different parts of the roots, trunk, branches, leaves, cones, fruit and seeds, and what these mean, or focusing on different trees and how the tree is a metaphor for their situation.

Step by step

1. Spread the pictures of different kinds of trees on a surface (e.g. table, floor).
2. While you are spreading the pictures, ask the client to connect to their breathing for a couple of breaths.
3. Invite the client to choose one picture that represents their ideal profesional 'identity'. Invite the client to consider their intuition, as well as their 'head'.
4. Help the client explore the picture they have chosen by asking questions, such as:
   a. What made you choose this picture?
   b. If your ideal professional identity were this tree:
      i. What would be your roots/trunk/branches/leaves/fruits/etc.?
      ii. What would you need to flourish (looking at the surroundings of the tree)?
   c. How do you feel now, when looking at this tree?
   d. How close are you now in resemblance to this tree? What do you already have in place?
5. And finally, you can ask the client: "What is the first step you need to take to grow your professional identity towards your vision?"
6. If they would like to, invite the client to take a picture of their tree, as a reminder.

Pirjo Puhakka is an executive coach, coaching supervisor, mentor coach and Henley tutor.

Crazy Eights

Ingredients

Paper (A3 or A4) and pen

When does it work best?

Crazy Eights is a very adaptable tool, which can help clients who feel they overthink things and would like to develop their flexibility. It is also useful for clients who feel stuck for new ideas or perspectives, as the rapid nature of the exercise encourages creativity and provides a choice of ways to access ideas.

Description

Crazy Eights is a flexible and creative tool to rapidly enable a client to gain different perspectives on an issue or to develop new ideas for a product, service or change in their lives. Originating in the design industry, it puts clients on the spot to respond creatively and spontaneously in the moment to question prompts related to the goal or theme of the coaching. Using one sheet of paper, a client generates eight images or responses in eight minutes before taking a step back to explore certain ideas or wider themes in more detail. The technique helps to free-up the mind and encourage flexible and playful engagement with a topic, which often leads to new insights and ideas.

Step by step

1. Give the client a piece of paper (A3 or A4) and ask them to fold it into eighths and then reopen it again so the folds are visible. Place the sheet vertically so the client has four pairs of horizontal boxes in front of them. Ideally, give them a felt-tip pen.
2. Explain that they will be asked to fill one box each minute in response to a question. This is likely to be an image but can contain text, and they should try and withhold judgement about the quality of their work.
3. Ensuring that you are clear about the goal they would like to work on, set a timer for one minute, ask the first question and press 'start'.
4. After one minute, instruct them to stop, immediately ask the next question and start the timer again. Repeat until all eight boxes are filled.
5. You have free rein to invent your own questions and have chance to do so in the one-minute gaps. Or you can simply ask them to come up with an idea a minute, in response to a design question or problem.
6. Here are some potential questions to prompt the generation of 'crazy eights', using an example of a client wishing to improve cross-organisation working within their work system:
   - What is the first thing that comes to mind when I mention the system?
   - What does happiness look like in the system?
   - How would your grandmother view (or have viewed) the system?
   - If there were no divisions within the system, what would it be like?
   - A computer programme is being made to help clients navigate the system. What does the homepage look like?
   - A film is being made about the story of your system. What's on the poster?
   - The system has had a great day. What does that look like for you?
   - Money is no object and anything is possible! What does that look like in the system?

Crazy Eights

7. Once the boxes have all been filled, ask them to reflect on their crazy eights and identify:
   - Which boxes stand out for them and why
   - Any wider themes or insights.
8. At this point, you can then continue the coaching conversation, supporting the client in their development of a specific idea or approach towards achieving their goal.

Julie Flower is a leadership and team development coach, consultant and facilitator, specialising in navigating uncertainty in complex systems and applied improvisation.

The Four 'P's

Ingredients

Paper and pen

When does it work best?

When a client is interested in a structure for evaluating the week gone by, as well as starting each week on the front foot. The framework provides a way of aligning experiences and expectations, and identifying intentions for the week ahead within different life domains. The framework embeds the coaching into a context of initial self-processing. The prerequisite is a self-driven client, motivated for doing work prior to sessions. It is also an advantage if the client already enjoys some form of writing or journaling.

Description

This tool creates opportunity for the client to reflect prior to a coaching session through a structured yet loose journaling process. It is a tool that structures an overview of experiences, thought patterns and progression. A key advantage is enabling different foci related to different domains of one's life, thus making reflection around one's life easier to manage/assess. The four 'P's represent different domains of the client's life:

- Private – relevant for a client individually (e.g. personal goals, aspirations, dreams, challenges);
- Personal – relevant in relation to personal relationships (e.g. friends, family, spouse);
- Professional – experiences in relation to the professional domain (e.g. career, business);
- Privilege – experiences that represent highlights; something one feel privileged to have experienced.

Besides an overview of the different contexts, the structure allows for both retrospective reflection/evaluation of the week gone by and prospective planning for the upcoming week. Thus it becomes possible to start the following week on the front foot. Of course, this entails that the client is interested and supported around integrating the tool as a weekly habit.

Step by step

1. Introduce the client to the framework; describe the four 'P's and the process, and show the template for how it can be filled out.
2. Invite the client to undertake the task as a homework task.
3. At the next session, invite the client to review the events of the past week with a calendar and their journaling at hand.
4. Invite the client to reflect on their experiences and to identify three elements they feel thankful for or *privileged* around. These can be anything, big or small, amongst what you've experienced. The important thing is that the elements make you feel grateful or privileged.
5. Turn to the week ahead. Look at what is coming up in the diary and invite the client to state their intentions for each of the remaining three 'P's (*private, personal, professional*). The point is not to state goals (which are more rigid), but to narrow your attention around what you set out to create.
6. Repeat this reflective process at each subsequent coaching session.

Johan Frederik Banzhaf is Henley coaching tutor in Denmark and supports leaders on ambitious adventures through a specialty in sustainable high performance.

Hypothesis Tree

Ingredients

Pens and Post-its

When does it work best?

Hypothesis trees work well when clients have a potential way forward that they would like to test, or when they are faced with a complex problem and limited time and resources in which to address it. The hypothesis tree can also be a useful way to bring an evidence-based perspective and challenge to a topic. The coach helps to shine a light on potential gaps and shortcomings in the evidence. The main pitfall of hypothesis trees is the risk of confirmation bias – the selection of evidence to support the argument. Challenge from the coach and an encouragement to consider alternative hypotheses can guard against this.

Description

A hypothesis tree is a way to explore and test assumptions, recommendations or decisions logically. It is a problem-solving tool in that it invites individuals to considers how much evidence is required to make a convincing case. The tool is used extensively in management consulting; it can be an efficient way to get to the heart of an issue and a compelling way to construct an argument. The tool enables the grouping of similar ideas and helps clients to structure their thinking, particularly in the case of complex, multi-faceted decisions, and promotes critical thinking. It starts with an assumption and then groups arguments and evidence beneath it in a logical and ordered way.

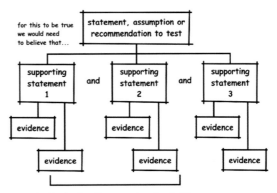

Step by step

1. The coach asks the client to identify a hypothesis (in the form of a statement) that they would like to test. The coach invites the client to write this on a Post-it note.
2. The coach then asks the client "what would need to be true in order for the hypothesis to stand?"
3. These ideas should be captured on Post-its and then grouped to form three or four themes (statements again) at the second level of the tree. For example, issues relating to capacity, resources and timing might fall naturally under a theme of 'It is feasible'.
4. The coach then explores each branch with the client by asking what evidence would be needed to make each thematic statement true and where that would be found, as well as what evidence would undermine the statement.
5. Exploration is likely to lead to action-planning around the collection and review of evidence; the refinement or complete rewriting of the hypothesis; and an improved awareness of the most important factors for the client in their decision-making.

Julie Flower is a leadership and team development coach, consultant and facilitator, specialising in navigating uncertainty in complex systems and applied improvisation.

Reframing

Ingredients

A clear mind

When does it work best?

When you notice your client is stuck in their own perspective of things.

Description

Often, clients are stuck in their own perspective of a situation. Their fixed perception of things prevents them from seeing new solutions, changing their behaviour or beliefs, and moving on. Reframing is an invitation to change this perspective and here are two ways to approach this. The first way is to ask your client to come up with alternative perceptions themselves. You do this by asking questions. The advantage is that the perceptions will be closer to the context of the client. The disadvantage is that the reframe may not go far enough to achieve a breakthrough. A second, and more invasive, way is that the coach offers alternative perceptions. The advantage is that the coach will have a different perspective, usually further away from what the client might come up with themself. The disadvantage is that the reframe may be too far off the world of the client and that it may affect the relationship in a negative way. Close rapport with your client is essential. It's important to note that the reframe in itself does not bring a solution. Its purpose is to provide a springboard from which to create movement to make progress in a new direction.

Reframing

Step by step

A) When you want the client to construct the reframe, you might ask questions like:
- "What other interpretations could you imagine of this event?"
- "How would Gandhi [or your boss, a coincidental bystander, etc.] react to this [or solve this or see this]?"

B) When you as a coach construct the reframe, here are four possible ways of doing this.

1. Change one or more words in the client perspective. For example:
    Client: "I hate my boss."
    Coach: "You have a difficult relationship with your boss."

2. Refocus the attention on the consequences of the statement. For example:
    Client: "I hate my boss."
    Coach: "These feelings will make it very difficult for you to perform in your job."

3. Focus the attention on the intention of the statement. For example:
    Client: "I hate my boss."
    Coach: "It's a good thing that you can express your feelings about your boss: now we have something to work with."

4. Chunk down the statement to decrease the size of the issue. For example:
    Client: "I hate my boss."
    Coach: "What does your boss specifically do that you don't like?"

Marc Innegraeve is a leadership and team coach. He trained at Henley Business School and works mostly in technology environments.

Hanuman Finds Lost Confidence

Ingredients

None

When does it work best?

This tool works best for clients who may be familiar with the story of Rama, and when the coach is aware of the client's past success, but due to present circumstances, the client may now lack the confidence to undertake the next challenge. Sometimes abusive leaders, negative work environments and personal experiences can impact on client confidence. This story can act as a catalyst for some clients, helping them connect with past successes and building confidence to move forward.

Description

According to the *Ramayana* (the holy scripture of Hindu religion), Lord Rama, his wife Goddess Sita, and his brother, Laxman, were exiled to the forest for 14 years. During this time, Goddess Sita was kidnapped by the demon king of Lanka, Ravana. When Rama and Laxman heard that Sita had been kidnapped they were alarmed. As they were far away, they asked Hanuman (a senior member of the monkeys' battalion in the forest) to go to Lanka and search for Goddess Sita. Hanuman saw the great distance between their location and Lanka, which was covered by a deep sea, and his courage failed him. It was then his friends reminded him of the strength he possessed when he was a child. They told him that during his childhood he could fly and could defeat animals including the biggest elephant. They told him that due to a saint's curse, he had forgotten all his powers to fly and conquer demons. This filled Hanuman with huge confidence and he flew to Lanka to search for Goddess Sita, and ultimately rescued her.

Step by step

1. Ask the client if they have heard of the *Ramayana* (Hindu holy scripture), Lord Rama, Goddess Sita and Hanuman.
2. Remind them of this episode in the *Ramayana*.
3. Remind the client of a previous conversation in which they described a past success.
4. Invite the client to share details of the experiences, including how the events may not have gone exactly to plan, but they were still able to adapt and succeed. Explore the factors which lead to this success.
5. Encourage them to talk about the feelings of achieving the successful outcome.
6. Explore the ways in which the client can draw on these insights to help them move forward in the present situation.
7. Invite the client to visualise a successful outcome.
8. Invite the client to visualise how they will manage (cope) when unforeseen events happen (as they did in the previous event).
9. Invite the client to formulate the insights from this discussion.
10. Explore a plan to move forward.

Badri Bajaj is a leading coach and researcher, and imparts coaching training to individuals and organisations.

Questions – If You Knew the Answer

Ingredients

None

Description

Good questions are the coach's best friend, in terms of engaging clients and subtly drawing curiosity and quality thought and discussion around specific topics. This technique is an approach that can be used at any point in a conversation when a client asks themselves a rhetorical question or is stuck in their thinking and cannot see beyond where they are – a relatively common occurrence when thoughts are spiralling round and round in a closed thinking loop. Nancy Kline describes the impact of this when exploring a person's 'thinking environment' (Kline, 1999), in terms of how often it can surprise the client that they in fact knew the answer and that it was, in some ways, simple.

When does it work best?

This works best during any reflective conversation and can lead to some surprising insights for your client. It is also a useful technique to adopt if you feel the conversation is stuck, or the client is making assumptions without questioning why, or believes there is no way past an obstacle. It works well because the nature of the question implies there is an already known solution. It's also a useful question if you, as coach, feel a little stuck with the conversation. A word of caution when using the approach is to ensure your client feels supported and not irritated by the questions so the coach should judge the level of rapport before using this approach or any of the following questions.

Step by step

1. A coach may often find themselves witnessing a client asking themselves a seemingly rhetorical question whilst they are talking. This provides an opportunity to ask them what they think the answer is. e.g from the client, 'I know what I want to achieve, but I don't know how my family would react to these changes – would they support me or would they feel I wasn't making the right choices?'
2. Coach then asks
   'and what is the answer to that question'
   or
   'I'm guessing you don't know the answer to that question right now, but what do you think it might be'
3. Coach can then follow this up with
   'and, if you did know the answer, what would it be?'

Questions – If You Know the Answer

Additional "unlocking questions" along the same lines include:

- *'What would be the best question I could ask you now?'*

This implies that there are many questions that could be asked and prompts the client to ask themselves the "best" one.

- *'If you secretly knew the way forward from here, what would it be?'*

This question assumes there is actually a way forward. It also assumes that they already somehow know it.

- *'If you were coaching yourself, what question would you ask now?'*

By asking your client to put their coaching hat on, you may get a surprisingly insightful question

- *'What question do YOU think I should ask you now?'*

By asking the question using the word 'should' you imply that you want to help them cut through all the complexity to help them move forwards

- *'I don't know where to go next with this. Where would you go?'*

If you're able to ask this question confidently, you can show them that they are the expert in their own subject matter and show empathy. It can sometimes give the client permission to lead down a path they felt nervous to explore or admit to being interested in.

References

Kline, N. (1999) *Time to Think*. London: Cassell.

Maggie Grieve combines 30 years of global business-development leadership experience, team and executive coaching accreditations and her passion for facilitating lasting, positive change to help individuals and teams succeed and be happy in life and business.

Attribution Styles

Ingredients

Pen/pencil and paper

Or flipchart marker and flipchart

Description

According to social psychology, attributions are inferences that we make about the causes of events, our behaviour, as well as the behaviour of others. Attributions help us understand the underlying 'why' and strongly influence our thoughts, feelings and behaviours. For the purpose of this exercise, we classify attributions along two dimensions: internal–external and stable–variable. In an internal attribution, we infer that an event outcome or a behaviour is caused by dispositional factors such as personal traits and abilities. In an external attribution, we believe that situational factors are at play. In a stable attribution, we assume that the underlying factors are stable and unchangeable, whereas in a variable attribution we assume that these factors are only of a temporary nature and thus changeable.

Our attribution style can significantly impact our sense of self-efficacy and our performance motivation, as well as our emotional reactions to successes and failures. Oftentimes, our attribution styles follow patterns (optimistic vs. pessimistic) and can also be subject to self-serving or hindering biases. To illustrate this, imagine your client has just won an important business contract following extensive negotiations and presentations. A self-supporting attribution could be as follows: "*I have great negotiation/presentation skills*" (internal) and "*I am using these skills in all of my client relationships*" (stable). A self-hindering attribution could be: "*I was lucky – the client made it easy for me*" (external) and "*I only did well in this specific situation*" (variable). In case of a failure scenario, self-supporting attributions would be external and variable, whereas self-hindering attributions would be internal and stable.

When does it work best?

The method works best in situations when the client would benefit from a change in perspective to better understand the true causes of events and behaviour. It also helps clients in adapting a more realistic and self-serving attribution style that enhances their sense of self-worth, self-efficacy and overall mood, without tipping into a state of arbitrary overconfidence.

Step by step

1. Provide some background information about the method.
2. Invite the client to think of a specific situation in which they have experienced either a success or a failure and ask them to assign a headline to that situation.

Attribution Styles

3. Invite the client to explore and elaborate on the different reasons that led to the specific outcome. Let them write down several reasons.
4. Then draw two lines, one underneath the other. Assign the category titles 'internal' and 'external' to the left and right ends of the first line. Assign 'stable' and 'variable' to those of the second line.
5. Invite the client to assign each of their reasons to the categories.
6. Invite the client to explore the patterns that unfold on the charts.
7. Suggest assessing different gradations along each of the two lines instead of focusing on 'black and white' categories.
8. Suggest the client explores what reasons could be available once they move from one category end (e.g. internal) to the other (e.g. external or vice versa).
9. Ask the client to summarise their conclusions with regard to the situation/event reviewed.

Sabine Renner is an organisational psychologist, certified coach and trainer who works at the intersection of leadership, personal development, neuroscience and positive psychology.

COATES

Ingredients

None

Description

With many hours in a week spent at work, the need for quality workplace connections is the foundation not only of wellbeing, but also of how you show up at and apply yourself to your work. COATES (**c**ompassion, **o**ptimism, **a**wareness, **t**rust, **e**motions and **s**trengths) provides a framework for coaches and clients to help understand what is happening in their workplace and personal relationships. While COATES may look stage-like, in fact it is a dynamic framework, whereby you can work on any one element at time. It is intended that each element influences the others.

In the first instance, the coach and, importantly, the client need to gain an understanding of the relationship challenge and what their part is within that challenge. Compassion enables forgiveness for themselves and others. Optimism requires some cognitive reframing through identifying what is working well amongst the negatives. Awareness is foundational to all coaching work. Becoming more aware of ourselves, our role and the possible experiences of others enables solid solution finding and the experience of empathy. Trust is foundational to the quality of relationships: it can easily be broken, but it provides the opportunity to grow and reset relationships; however, it requires awareness and intentional actions. The various emotions at play should be explored, along with how they are influencing the client's capacity to think and move forward, or even accept. Strengths identification is confidence building and supports action planning to foster valued workplace and personal relationships.

An understanding of what each component brings to the relationship and careful attention to the coaching relationship, to mirror COATES at its best, are imperative to a good coaching outcome for the client. The relationship brings with it a space in which the client can experience COATES, learn and then replicate it in their workplace relationships.

When does it work best?

This coaching technique works best when a client feels disconnected from their colleagues or has had a rupture in a workplace relationship and feels uncertain as to how to reconnect or heal and revitalise the relationship. Clients will often feel vulnerable; hence the coaching relationship needs to be strong and exhibiting all factors of COATES so as to increase the client's sense of psychological safety and coaching effectiveness. COATES can also be useful when teams are forming or there are struggles within already formed teams.

Step by step

1. Explain COATES and its parts to the client.
2. Explore how their workplace relationship fits in each part of COATES.
3. Using a scale of 0–5 (where 0 = non-existent, 5 = highly satisfying), ask the client to rate each part of COATES currently.
4. Ask the client or team on what part of COATES they would like to focus their coaching:
a. Exploring the relationships at work
b. Exploring each element of COATES (compassion, optimism, awareness, trust, emotions and strengths)
c. Exploring the impact of COATES on the client's capacity to change or identify new thoughts and behaviours
d. Supporting the client as they develop preferred actions and an implementation plan.

Wendy-Ann Smith is an accredited coaching psychologist, author, inquisitive travelling photographer and mum of one.

The Inner Team

Ingredients

Chairs or Post-it notes

When does it work best?

The method works best in situations when the client is facing conflicting perspectives that need to be integrated to create congruence.

Reference

Schulz von Thun, F. (2004) *Das Innere Team In Aktion*. Rowohlt Taschenbuch Verlag.

Sabine Renner is an organisational psychologist, certified coach and trainer who works at the intersection of leadership, personal development, neuroscience and positive psychology.

Description

The Inner Team method was originally developed by Friedemann Schulz von Thun (2004), who said: "If you want to be a good communicator, look inside yourself first". He used the metaphor of the inner team to describe the various inner voices that we carry within ourselves, like the two souls in our breast that are often at odds with each other and send us very different messages. The inner team consists of various team members who possess individual characteristics and have different perspectives on the topic at hand. Some of these team members get along with each other well; others might be in looming conflict or are even fighting with each other. Some are rather loud and very visible, while others keep a low profile. The better the team members cooperate with each other and are able to integrate contrary opinions, the easier and less energy consuming it becomes to make clear and congruent decisions and communicate and follow through accordingly.

The inner team is led by the client themselves, who is responsible for showing an interest in and appreciating each team member's perspective, and for consolidating these in congruent and clear solutions. In the exercise, each voice or perspective can be represented by a chair or Post-it note (depending on the space available).

Step by step

1. Provide some background information about the method.
2. Ask the client what topic (e.g. a decision to be made) they want to focus on.
3. Ask the client to identify the team members who should be considered in this decision-making process. Remind them that these team members are not actual colleagues but rather inner voices. Ask them not only to focus on the obvious, loud team members but also to check whether additional 'voices' should be heard.
4. Invite the client to enter into an inner dialogue (i.e. provide a space for them to listen to these inner voices). For each of these self-created team members, let the client listen to what the member has to say and then define the key message. Ask them to assign a nickname – for example, 'the perfectionist', 'the concerned', 'the achiever'. Once the inner team is complete, ask the client whether any member is still missing. Who else might be interested in having a say?
5. Ask the client to moderate a dialogue between the different team members and to watch out for conflicts as well as agreements that arise. Ask them to structure the different perspectives.
6. Ask the client what kind of solution they could envision that would address the majority of the different team members' concerns. Let the client present the solution and negotiate with the team members to define a congruent solution.

Emotional Intelligence (EQ/EI)

Ingredients

An emotional intelligence assessment, 360 report or perceptions of EQ

When does it work best?

Emotional intelligence tools can deliver the highest value with a client who is low on self-awareness, but they are also useful for those looking to develop greater influencing and wider leadership skills. As with most tools, the intervention works best when the client is motivated to change and interested in exploring how this idea can help them achieve their wider personal, leadership or career goals.

Description

Emotional intelligence (EQ, also known as EI) has been argued to be more important than IQ for leaders. While IQ may help individuals progress to middle-management roles, EQ can help them build the relationships and networks that are key in the journey from manager to leader. Although EQ has become popular in recent decades, it is not a new idea. Edward Thorndike (1927) coined the term 'social intelligence', meaning a person's ability to understand and manage other people, and to engage in adaptive social interactions, to understand and relate to others. This work has been further developed by Daniel Goleman, who helped to popularise emotional intelligence (Goleman et al., 2003). Goleman defined six leadership styles: commanding, visionary, affiliative, democratic, pacesetting and coaching. Alongside these, Goleman suggested that successful leaders manage five key elements – self-awareness, self-regulation, motivation, empathy and social skills – as they interact with others using the six leadership styles. Helping managers and leaders to understand their emotions and work with them is the focus of this tool. One way to do this is through the wide number of EQ questionnaires that are published by test providers. Training and accreditation are essential to ensure ethical practice.

Step by step

1. If you plan to use a psychometric assessment, first discuss and agree how the test will be carried out. Encourage your client to be in a 'normal' frame of mind when they complete their assessment: if they are feeling particularly stressed, this can show up in their responses and distort the report that follows. At the very least, they should be aware of their feelings and situation whilst completing the questions.
2. Understand the source of data around your client's EQ. If this is the perceptions of others, perhaps in a 360 report, check that this has been shared openly with your client. If it hasn't, suggest that this should happen prior to the coaching session starting. It is also important to try to get more details about what lies behind these perceptions, especially examples of situations that can be worked on with your client.
3. As usual, a three-way discussion with your client and their sponsor is helpful. This also avoids the coach being the one to introduce surprises to the client.
4. If a psychometric assessment has been used, you should read the report carefully before your client sees it, perhaps making notes about possible questions for your client.
5. It is highly advisable to talk through a psychometric report with the client before sending it to them. This provides an opportunity to observe their responses as they encounter the feedback for the first time. It also provides a space for questions based on these immediate reactions.

Emotional
Intelligence
(EQ/EI)

6. Invite your client to consider the information, and its implications for their role and future development. This often leads to rich conversations, where past events and stories are explored and new insights gained.
7. Share the report with the client for further reflection.
8. The report can also provide a platform for future coaching sessions or for a tool to track change.

References

Goleman, D., Boyatzis, R., and Mckee, A. (2003) *The New Leaders: Transforming the Art of Leadership into the Science of Results.* New York: Sphere.

Thorndike, E.L. (1927) *The Measurement of Intelligence.* New York: Bureau of Publications, Teacher's College, Columbia University.

Phil Summerfield is an experienced executive and executive coach helping leaders to become the people and the leaders they want to be.

Warren Buffet Method 2.0

Ingredients

Pen/pencil and paper

Or flipchart marker and flipchart

When does it work best?

The method works best in situations when the client already has clarity about their existing goals but has difficulties in prioritising these. The method also helps to create a coherent and aligned goal structure, identifying a common vision or direction, and clarifying the time horizon for each of these goals.

Reference

Duckworth, A. (2016) *GRIT: The Power of Passion and Persistence.* New York: Scribner Book Company.

Sabine Renner is an organisational psychologist, certified coach and trainer who works at the intersection of leadership, personal development, neuroscience and positive psychology.

Description

The Warren Buffet Method of goal prioritisation is a simple yet profound method that helps clients move from a state of 'goal prioritisation overwhelm' to clarity and focus. It is said that investment manager Warren Buffet once asked his pilot whether he had professional dreams other than flying and then guided him through a simple three-step process to prioritise his goals and focus on those that truly mattered to him. The method outlined below is inspired by this story and further developed by Angela Duckworth (2016).

Step by step

1. Provide some background information about the method.
2. Ask the client to prepare an inventory of all the business or career goals they want to accomplish, the projects they want to move forward and the ideas they are eager to pursue.
3. Let the client define which of these goals is truly meaningful and important – at most, this should be five goals. Ask the client whether these goals are – ideally – serving one common, overarching professional vision that points in a clear direction.
4. Point the client to the remaining goals on the list. Are these somehow contributing to the achievement of the top-level goals, so that they function as a means to an end? If that is the case, ask the client to add these mean-goals to their goal hierarchy so that these lower-level goals support and lead to the top-level goals. By doing so, they not only create a coherent goal structure but also clarify the intermediate goals that contribute to the achievement of the most important goals.
5. Ask the client to assess how these goals interlink with each other from a timing perspective. How are these goals building upon each other? What needs to happen first so that something else can be moved forward? In case of limited time resources and to avoid overwhelm, what needs to be put on hold, at least temporarily?
6. If any goals are left on your client's initial list, ask them to avoid working on these at all costs. Help them to say 'no' to the good in order to embrace the great and focus on a set of consciously chosen and aligned goals.
7. Finally, ask your client to define and commit to a plan of actionable first steps and the respective timeline for these.

Grey Thinking for Thinking Errors

Ingredients

Pen and paper

When does it work best?

This tool works well as homework after a session where the coach has identified the use of several thinking errors. Thinking errors might immobilise the client, or make them move in a direction they would not if they knew their thinking was not reality. The tool allows the client to think of next steps once they have looked at the other extreme and the greys.

Description

Cognitive Behavioural Therapy has classified extreme, illogical and inaccurate thinking as thinking errors. Thinking errors may cause stress, anxiety and sadness, among other emotions. Common thinking errors include:

- *Mind reading (jumping to conclusions)*: this is making conclusions without having all the information, for example: "People who do not know me well think I have no expertise when they hear me talk."
- *All-or-nothing thinking:* looking at a situation from one extreme, for example: "Since I came back, I have lost all my expertise. This makes me a terrible manager." A common clue is the use of words such as 'awful', 'excellent', 'always', 'all', 'none' and 'never'.
- *Blame*: putting all responsibility on someone or something else without acknowledging how the person has contributed to the problem, for example: "I cannot work with my team: they are ignoring me, they are treating me as an outsider."
- *Personalisation*: taking things personally, for example: "My team is under-performing because of me. I do not have enough time for them."
- *Fortune-telling*: thinking you know what the future holds, for example: "I won't like that role."
- *Emotional reasoning*: using feelings as facts, for example: "I feel horrible when talking to new people, they probably don't like me."
- *Minimisation*: giving less value or importance to one's participation, for example: "They did not give me any negative feedback: they must have felt sorry for me because it was my first day."
- *Magnification*: seeing things worse than they really are, blowing things out of proportion, for example: "I handled that meeting terribly; they will never respect me as a manager."
- *Labelling*: attaching a label to yourself, for example: "I am such a failure."
- *Demands*: being inflexible with yourself. Clues are words such as 'should', 'have to', 'must', for example: "I have to know everything better than my team because I am their manager."
- *Low frustration tolerance*: believing you cannot deal with or handle a situation, for example: "I cannot stand working in such an environment." One clue is using the phrase 'I can't stand it'.
- *Phoneyism*: also called Impostor Syndrome, this is thinking that people will find out you are not what they think, for example: "I don't understand how that program works – my team will see that I don't know as much as a I should and that I got here by luck" (Palmer and Whybrow, 2019).

This tool invites the client to write down their thinking errors, to think of the other extreme, and then to explore what a middle ground would be. After looking at the extremes and the middle ground, the client can think about how to achieve the desired state.

Grey Thinking for
Thinking Errors

Step by step

1. During the session, identify thinking errors as they arise.
2. Write them down on a table (see example below).
3. Invite the client to write down what the other extreme might be, as well as greys (i.e. thinking that is in the middle of the two extremes).
4. Invite the client to rank these thoughts, depending on which they feel impacts them the most negatively.
5. With the client, review alternative creative ways of acting differently and steps they might take.

Table: Grey Thinking

Extreme A	Grey	Extreme B	Priority	How to make it a Grey
People who do not know me well, think I have no expertise when they hear me talk.	Some people who do not know me well might think I have no expertise, but others give me the benefit of the doubt.	People who do not know me think I am an expert.	3	a. Think that there are both types of people in the room. b. Try seeing how I feel if I say: "When in the company of people I do not know, I say out loud my concern, that maybe they think I have no expertise, but that actually people who know me… etc." c. Ask people who have known me for a while how they felt about me when they first got to know me. d. Ask my manager what people have told her.
I feel like an outsider; my team is ignoring me.	My team feels confident to make decisions but come to me for input when needed.	I am the centre of my team; the team runs every-thing by me.	1	Arrange regular check-ins. Have a process for new or ad hoc tasks: 1. Have a meeting about what needs to be done 2. They write a proposal with a checklist 3. They check-in as they work 4. There is a final review. For the bread and butter issues, they tell me about it in our one-to-one meetings, unless something changes direction, in which case they call me. Book time in my diary for them to know that they can call me.

Extreme A	Grey	Extreme B	Priority	How to make it a Grey
I have to know everything better than my team. a. This makes me a terrible manager.	a. I know, on a high level, everything my team does and I have expertise on the most important bits. b. I support my team and have lots of experience in the company, which allows me to be a good manager.	a. I am an expert b. I am an excellent manager.	2	a. I will ask my team to invite me to meetings where they explain to external users about the new tools so that I learn about them. b. I will use my strengths in my management, like my attention to detail and long-term thinking.
I have to know everything better than my team because I am their manager.	I need to understand on some level most of the things my team do and I need to have expertise on some things.	I don't need to have expertise – that is why I have a team.	4	Ask my team to make a list of everything they do. Together with my manager, make a prioritisation to learn about the things my team does and decide what level of expertise I need.

6. Close the session as you would normally do, inviting the client to consider what their next step will be. How do they plan to go about it? When do they think they will take this first step? Is there anything that might get in the way? How do they think they will feel after they take this step? Is there anything that could support them in taking it?

Reference

Palmer, S., and Whybrow, A. (eds) (2019) *Handbook of Coaching Psychology: A Guide for Practitioners* (2nd edition). London: Routledge.

Claudia Day is an accredited coach and entrepreneur with a marketing strategy background, and trained in coaching at Henley Business School and management at MIT Sloan.

Changing the Script

Ingredients

Pen and paper

When does it work best?

The tool is most helpful when a client keeps slipping into old conversational habits and struggles to change a pattern of recurring conversations, despite knowing it won't end well. It is particularly helpful for tackling the obstructive cycle of conversation, which has become a habit they feel unable to change and which leads to negative, unproductive dialogue.

Description

This tool helps clients to change the unhelpful conversation patterns that keep reoccurring in similar situations in their life. These conversations are usually between the client and significant other individuals with whom they have frequent interaction. Clients can often recognise the pattern and can foresee that the conversation is likely to end negatively, but feel stuck and unable to change the groundhog-day outcome. This tool encourages clients to change the script and break the cycle of negative conversation habits. It can help them to get unstuck and make a positive change by guiding them through the conversation, part by part. It does this by offering time and space to consider alternatives and build a new, constructive pattern in a safe environment.

Step by step

1. Invite the client to describe the conversation that they have identified as often slipping into a negative, dysfunctional pattern.
2. Help them relive the most recent occurrence of that conversation and, as they speak, make a note of the 'script' using the table below.

What did the client say?	What did the other person say?	What did the client feel?

3. Invite the client to select one point in the conversation/script they would like to change.
4. Explore with the client what change they could make and how this change could be made.
5. Invite the client to select another point in the conversation/script they would like to change.
6. Explore with the client again what change they could make and how this change could be made.
7. Continue until the client is satisfied with the changed script. Once they are satisfied that the script is changed to an adequate level, encourage them to try this new script when the conversation next happens and they feel they are slipping into old habits.

Jelena Jovanovic Moon is a Henley-trained coach and psychologist with degrees in coaching and organisational change and senior leadership roles in people management and organisational development.

VIP – Ask the Expert

Ingredients

None needed

When does it work best?

It works best if your client is stuck or lacking ideas. They might be feeling out of their depth or lacking prior experience or inner resources. They might say "I don't know what else I could do."

Description

There is plenty of opportunity to get creative with this technique for generating ideas. Let your client's imagination get to work. Sometimes clients have a limited bank of experiences or resources to draw upon. They might not have been in a certain kind of situation before or they might have tried several things that haven't worked and come to a dead end. This activity is a great way of having some fun by introducing advice from others who aren't present. Who else might be the expert in this situation and what wisdom do they offer? You will be asking your client to step out of their own shoes and into those of someone they admire. This could be an expert in the same field, a family member, a historical figure, a character from literature or a celebrity (Passmore and Sinclair, 2020). The creative opportunities are limitless.

Step by step

1. Establish the situation your client would like to explore.
2. Capture their initial ideas for making progress, solving the problem or creating change.
3. When they have run out of their own ideas or possibilities, ask them for the names of three people they admire. Explain that these could be historical figures, celebrities, sports people, a family member, a cartoon character or anyone else. If you have lots of time available, extend your list to five people.
4. Take the first person on the list. Get your client to imagine by asking: "What would this person do themselves if they were in the same situation?" "What would this person be saying to themselves about this situation, in order to solve it, make it better or achieve what they want?" "What would this person be saying to other people if they were in this situation?"
5. Repeat as above for the other people on the list. Reassure the client that this stage is for generating ideas and insights – all ideas and thoughts are potentially useful.
6. By now, you should have a wonderful collection of possible behaviours, skills, capabilities, solutions, strategies, ideas and so on. What has your client learnt from the people they admire? Help your client to sort through them and prioritise what they might take forward themselves. Create practical steps and actions.

Reference

Passmore, J., and Sinclair, T. (2020) *Becoming a Coach: The Essential ICF Guide.* Worthing: Pavilion Publishing.

Clare Smale is an accredited coach, supervisor and author who runs her own business, inspired2learn.

The Five Whys

Ingredients

Pen and paper

Description

The Five Whys tool originated from the Toyota Production System, where it was used to solve problems in the manufacturing world, focusing on an in-depth understanding of shop-floor issues rather than assumptions made by management. In a coaching context, the tool helps clients in their decision-making process by dissecting their motivation in regards to the action they feel uncertain about. By asking "why?" five times, the coach helps the client to drill down into their driving forces and authentic reasons for action.

The tool comprises a sequence of 'why' questions that the coach guides the client through. Although "why?" seems like a simple question, its answer requires serious thinking on the part of the client. Each answer forms the basis of the next question and, paradoxically, the questions themselves are the answers. It is a questioning process that gets to the bottom of the issue. The coach begins with the question "Why do you want to do this?" and keeps asking "why?" until the client reveals a complete picture, as opposed to what simply lies on the surface of their motivation. The notion is that initially presented problems are just symptoms of deeper issues. Making a decision based on an initial response may offer a quick solution, but it won't provide understanding of the core drivers and consequently may not help a client solve to their dilemma. This sequence of 'why' questions almost always leads to deeper reflection and awareness of a client's motives, values and underlying self-identity. As a result, the client is able to make the decision.

When does it work best?

This is a simple but powerful tool because it cuts through superficial causes, shifts aside symptoms and gets to the root of an issue. It can therefore be used whenever a client feels overwhelmed, unable to make a decision or is moving to the action stage. It helps them break down the set of obstacles that prevent the clarity necessary for decision-making. It does this by helping them dig deeper and deeper into the real drivers of their motivation. It is very helpful for cases when a client needs further clarity on what really matters to them. The newly gained clarity also results in strong motivation for action. What the tool does is to effectively enable the client to make an informed decision. This simple technique can often direct a client quickly to the root cause of their inner conflict. Its simplicity offers great flexibility of application.

Step by step

1. Invite the client to think about the question "Why do I want to take this action?" and note down their answers. For example:
    Question: "Why do I want to take this job?"
    Answer: "To progress in my career."

The Five Whys

2. Refer to the client's answer and ask them to think "Why do I want to take this action?" For example:
    Question: "Why do I want to progress in my career?"
    Answer: "To be better qualified and gain more skills."

3. Refer to the client's answer again and ask them to think "Why do I want to take this action?" For example:
    Question: "Why do I want to be better qualified and gain more skills?"
    Answer: "To have a wider choice of possible future jobs."

4. Refer to the client's answer again and ask them to think "Why do I want to take this action?" For example:
    Question: "Why do you want to have wider choice of possible future jobs?"
    Answer: "To avoid being stuck doing the same thing for 30 more years."

5. Refer to the client's answer again and ask them to think "Why do I want to take this action?" For example:
    Question: "Why do you need to avoid being stuck doing the same thing for 30 more years?"
    Answer: "To live an interesting, exciting, varied life and always have a choice."

The number 'five' in Five Whys is really just a rule of thumb. In some cases, you may have to ask 'why' a few more times, or a few less, before the client gets to the root of their motivation for their decision-making. Be mindful of this and recognise that the point to stop asking "why?" is when the client stops producing responses that are useful for their decision-making.

Invite the client to consider what they will do next and to discuss the action plan.

Jelena Jovanovic Moon
is a Henley-trained coach and psychologist with degrees in coaching and organisational change and senior leadership roles in people management and organisational development.

Naikan

Ingredients

Client notebook or paper and pen

When does it work best?

The technique can be used in one-to-one coaching to guide a client through the process of reflection or as part of a daily self-reflection practice by the coach or the client.

Description

'Naikan' means 'looking inside', although perhaps a more expressive definition would be 'seeing oneself with the mind's eye'. It was originally developed by Ishin Yoshimoto (1916–88) from the Japanese practice of *mishirabe* and is grounded in reality and the fundamental nature of the human condition. Naikan helps people to develop a stronger awareness of their own experiences through daily life, to reflect on their achievement of goals and to consider their relationships with themselves and others. Naikan helps clients bring their attention to the things that go unnoticed in the cut and thrust, through a compassionate approach to self-reflection. Whilst other techniques also offer a portal to generative change, Naikan is a very simple method that clients can use to deepen the quality of the relationship they have with themselves and others.

Step by step

1. Invite the client to bring to mind a specific person and context, either in the past or in the present.
2. Invite them to reflect on the list of answers to the following three questions:
   - What have you received from this person?
   - What have you given to this person?
   - What troubles or difficulties have you caused this person?
3. Review the answers – one list per question – to identify:
   - What lessons are now available?
   - What new awareness do you now have?
   - What has been taken for granted?
   - What do you need to do?
   - What do you need to do differently?
4. Invite the client to capture notes from their reflections.
5. The client should commit to the actions that need to be undertaken as a result of the answers given. Break down actions as much as you can and decide on completion dates.

Paul Crick helps ambitious businesses to reinvent and develop their leadership culture and leaders to become better ancestors to future generations.

Sensory Delights

Ingredients

None

When does it work best?

The tool works well when working with clients who are experiencing mild depression or are struggling to find joy in work. It is also helpful for clients who spend time in excessive rumination or catastrophising about possible future events. The tool aims to direct attention to the aspects of life that give each client pleasure and to find ways these aspects can be accentuated in their life, spending more time in the present and less time in the past or future.

Jonathan Passmore is a chartered psychologist, accredited coach, supervisor and director of the Henley Centre for Coaching, Henley Business School.

Description

Sensory awareness is being aware of the diverse sensory information that bombards us each day. When our minds are trapped in the past, ruminating about what has happened, or escape to the future, catastrophising about what is about to be, we lose touch with the present moment. Nurturing our ability to bring sensory experiences to the forefront of consciousness can enable clients to spend more time in the present moment and to direct such present-moment attention to aspects of life that delight them. In doing so, we can help clients create the space in the mind that allows them to stop and smell the roses, or taste the strawberries.

Step by step

1. The coach creates five columns on a piece of paper and labels each with one of the five senses: touch, taste, smell, sight and sound.
2. The coach invites the client to take ten minutes to think about and write down the experiences that give them pleasure through each of their senses. This can be set as a homework task at the end of a session.
3. The coach invites the client to discuss how specific experiences give them pleasure. The following can be useful questions to consider:
   - What surprised you about your lists?
   - Which of the items on your list do you experience every day?
   - As you reflect on the list, which items provide pleasure, comfort or enjoyment in each category?
   - How can you increase the number of experiences that give you pleasure, comfort and enjoyment each week?
   - How can you arrange your day to experience at least one source of sensual pleasure from each sense every day?

Osborn's Checklist (SCAMPER)

Ingredients

Pen and Post-it notes (using one Post-it per idea)

References

Eberle, B. (1982) *Visual Thinking: A 'Scamper' Tool for Useful Imaging*. New York: DOK Publishers.

Osborn, A. (1988) *Applied Imagination* (3rd edition). New York: Scribners.

Marc Innegraeve is a leadership and team coach, trained at Henley Business School and works mostly in technology environments.

Description

Most coaching clients can come up with a few ideas during a session to deal with their issues or challenges. Sometimes as a coach we may wish to encourage them to think more broadly. Osborn (1988) and Eberle (1982) created checklists to stimulate broader thinking. The term 'SCAMPER' is a mnemonic that can help by exploring ideas that **s**ubstitute, **c**ombine, **a**dapt, **m**inify/magnify, **p**ut to other uses, **e**liminate, **r**everse.

Step by step

Here are some sample questions for each element on the checklist. Obviously, these are examples and, as a coach, you will have to adapt to the situation and interaction with your client.

Substitute
- *What/who/where else instead? What else (process, material, resources…) could you do or use to achieve the same result?*

Combine
- *Could you combine ideas? What could you combine this with to make it better/stronger/more acceptable/more motivating…? How could you blend this with your context?*

Adapt
- *Can you adapt your idea to make it better/stronger/more acceptable/more motivating…? What actions/ideas from the past could you adapt to fit to your current situation? What solutions from others could you adapt to fit your need?*

Minify/Magnify
- *Could you make it smaller? What would happen if you made it fewer in numbers/scale/size…? What if you could reduce it to almost nothing?*
- *How big can you make it? What would be your most exaggerated version of this? What if you did this times 100/1,000/…? What would you do if your challenge was 1,000 times bigger?*

Put to other uses
- *Could you put your resources to other uses? What other things could you do with this idea?*

Eliminate
- *What could you leave out? What can you ignore? Where can you cut things away?*

Reverse
- *How can you make it worse? What would happen if you did the opposite? Can you do the same thing backwards? Could you turn the table around?*

Out of the Trenches

Ingredients

A chart to log the activities done by the client to help them select a prompt (optional)

When does it work best?

This tool works best where a strong working alliance has already been forged with the coach. The coach can share what they have noticed and then facilitate the client's thinking about behavioural patterns, through naming or feeding-back behaviours.

Description

This tool was developed with a client who reflected that after a big life change, she was now finally happy but often forgot that she was, finding herself using 'old' thinking patterns and behaviours. She described the situation as behaving as if she were still in the trenches, when in fact the battle was over. This tool is based on micro-practices, such as the practice from healthcare where health visitors encourage their clients to remember to do their pelvic-floor exercises when touching water. The client can choose a prompt (an event that happens several times a day) by thinking of activities they do several times a day, such as picking up keys, putting the kettle on, making a phone call or stroking the dog.

The client referred to this as "the trenches process" and expressed the value of stopping to ask herself how she is feeling and whether she is behaving in accordance with how she feels now, in order to change behaviour around self-image and confidence. Others have used the process to self-scan for behaviours they felt were problematic, including shallow breathing and intrusive thoughts.

Step by step

1. The coach notices the thinking pattern or behaviour.
2. The coach reflects back what the client has said.
3. The client may recognise this pattern, or may not.
4. If the latter, the coach could choose to gently challenge them, if the pattern feels important or relevant.
5. Further exploration often leads to an "Ah yes, I do!" moment.
6. The coach shares the concept of thinking patterns and pattern interruption.
7. Collaboratively, the coach and client consider how the client can notice a pattern and remind themselves to think about or reframe their current situation.
8. The client chooses an external trigger to encourage them to spot check themselves on whether they have been behaving as if they were still in the trenches.
9. The coach facilitates the client in keeping track and reflecting on whether the tool works.

Alex Porter is a Henley coach and trainer, specialising in behavioural change and habits. She previously worked as a teacher and support worker for women in prison.

Positive Case Conceptualisation

Ingredients

Whiteboard or paper and pen

References

Lane, D., and Corrie, S. (2009) Does Coaching Psychology Need the Concept of Formulation? *International Coaching Psychology Review*, 4(2), 193–206.

Passmore, J., and Oades, L.G. (2015) Positive Psychology Coaching Techniques: Positive Case Conceptualisation. *The Coaching Psychologist*, 11(1), 43–5.

Jonathan Passmore is a chartered psychologist, accredited coach, supervisor and director of the Henley Centre for Coaching, Henley Business School.

Description

The concept of case conceptualisation is derived from therapy and is commonly used in Cognitive Behavioural Therapy. Case conceptualisation is the formation of a rationale and framework, underpinned by an evidence base, to summarise the coaching thinking and inform future work with the client. Pioneered in coaching by David Lane and Sarah Corrie (2009), the tool can help coaches to formulate an evidenced-based approach to address client issues. The diagram illustrates how, together, the coach and client can create a shared understanding of the key challenges faced by the client and their relationships. The aim is not to 'diagnose' by finding causes, connections and possibilities, but instead to use positive case conceptualisation to refocus the approach towards new opportunities. One key guiding question when using the tool is *"if things are functioning really well, and people in the system are feeling good, what does it look like?"* Hence, whilst the coaching may be triggered by a problem, difficulty or transition, the positive case conceptualisation refocuses the client's thinking towards solutions, not problems. By using different colours, this positive mind map can be further enhanced.

Step by step

1. Invite the client to start talking about the challenges they face and to capture each significant aspect on a mind map.
2. They may wish to use pictures or different colours to represent different aspects, or simply words.
3. Invite the client to see the connections between elements – and to label these connections as you talk.
4. As the map develops with the key factors, encourage the client to start thinking about solutions and opportunities that may present themselves as they look at the emerging map.
5. When the map is completed, it can form the basis (or agenda) for future coaching work together.
6. At each session, the coach can invite the client: "Which aspect of the map would you like to focus on today?"
7. With each session, the client can add further opportunities, actions and solutions to the developing map.

Peak Moment

Ingredients

Pen and paper
(optional)

Description

This is a strength-based coaching technique that also helps clients to think about their values. Research confirms that working on our strengths provides much stronger motivation than working on our weaknesses. This tool draws on Abraham Maslow's concept of peak experience, an experience of the highest happiness and fulfilment, an event that happens when we are functioning at our most optimal level (Maslow, 1970). The tool encourages clients to think about those moments in life when they were at their very best, absorbed in the moment that made them feel absolutely fulfilled and at one with themselves, others and the world. By guiding a client through a peak moment in their life, when they felt they reached their full potential, a coach is helping them to identify key strengths that took them there and key values that drove them to success. As a result, this newly gained clarity should bring to light their core values, help them to make decisions on current matters, and provide a boost in self-esteem and the reassurance that they can cope with new coming challenges. Such peak moments become an anchor they can return to when their confidence drops and a reminder to them of what really matters and what they are capable of achieving.

When does it work best?

This tool is useful at times when a client is about to make a significant decision in their life (e.g. change of job/career, lifestyle, business endeavour, move, etc.). It helps them to identify their key values, which can shed light on what really matters to them and what made them successful and fulfilled in their life so far. Clients find it helpful to recall these peak moments consciously, and to remind themselves of their own resourcefulness and achievements. The tool provides the clarity necessary for decision-making, and increases their self-belief and motivation for action.

Step by step

1. Invite the client to think about a peak moment in their life (i.e. an event when they felt at the top of the world, content and at ease with everything in life). Examples include attaining a great achievement, finishing an important task, delivering exceptional performance, creating something new/innovative, playing an instrument or sport to an outstanding standard and building something of which they were proud. It could equally be a moment when they were doing routine tasks, but felt like that moment was so fulfilling. Whatever they choose, it should be a moment when their life felt meaningful and they felt truly themselves. Allow the client time to recall this moment and ask them to tell you when they have thought of it.

Peak Moment

2. Encourage the client to tell their story. Verbal attentions and questions help clients tell their story and bring the full memory to light. Questions might include:
   - Tell me about this moment – what is happening, what are you doing?
   - Where are you? What is around you?
   - Who else is with you?
   - What else do you notice?
   - What makes this such a special experience for you, why is it so important?

   Encourage the client to take couple of minutes to re-experience the moment.

3. Explore the experience in more depth. Questions here might include:
   - We talked about what you are doing, but how are you feeling in this moment?
   - What (if anything) are you saying to yourself?
   - What do you believe about yourself in this moment?
   - What is important and meaningful to you in this moment? What values drove you in this moment?

4. Move into 'lessons learnt' for the present. Questions might include:
   - How did you see yourself differently during your peak moment?
   - What did you believe about yourself, the world, your life in that peak moment?
   - What about now, as you look back:
     o What changed in you as a result of your peak moment?
     o How did your peak moment affect how you see your life now?
   - What was it that you valued highly at that moment (why it was so powerful and meaningful for you)? Why is each of these values important to you?

5. Invite the client towards a conclusion. Questions at this stage might include:
   - What is possible for you in life?
   - Who are you underneath it all, when all self-criticism, judgement and fear are taken away?
   - What are the positives about yourself that summarise the learning you had from this experience?
   - What can you carry forward into the rest of your life from this experience?

6. Invite the client to consider insights and future actions.

Reference

Maslow, A.H. (1970) Religious Aspects of Peak-experiences. In Sadler, W.A. (ed.) *Personality and Religion*. New York: Harper & Row.

Jelena Jovanovic Moon is a Henley-trained coach and psychologist with degrees in coaching and organisational change and senior leadership roles in people management and organisational development.

The Four Worlds of Existence

Ingredients

Diagram of the four worlds

When does it work best?

The model is best utilised at the beginning of a coaching relationship, but may inform the coach at every step of the coaching process.

Description

The Four Worlds Model (van Deurzen, 2012) is a cross-cultural map of interconnected dimensions within which we experience the world. It helps the coach to get a holistic sense of their client. Each dimension illustrates key aspects of the human experience based on the four fundamental existential tensions every client inevitably faces as a result of being alive and in the world with others. These can be explored through questions in a coaching session (Jacob, 2019).

The physical world (Umwelt)

Key questions: How does this client manage their physical space? How do they relate to their office or home environment, climate or geography? How do they experience their physical connection with the world (their body, health or level of fitness)?

The tension in this dimension is between striving to achieve safety and comfort while being faced with our physical limitations (the ultimate one being our inevitable physical demise).

The social world (Mitwelt)

Key questions: How does the client relate to other people? How do they experience themselves within their social and professional circles, their community and the culture(s) that surround them? How do they experience belonging, rejection and conflict?

The tension here relates to our innate need to belong and our desire to be different.

The psychological or personal world (Eigenwelt)

Key questions: How does this client define their character and identity? How do they relate to their thoughts and emotions, past experiences and future possibilities? What's their sense of integrity and authenticity? How do they experience freedom and responsibility?

The tension here is often experienced in the context of strengths and weaknesses or conflicting wants and needs when faced with difficult choices.

The spiritual world (Überwelt)

Key questions: What are the client's core values? How do they make sense of the world and their existence in it? What are their (spiritual) beliefs, ethics and morals? How do they manage experiences of absurdity and meaninglessness?

The tension here refers to our innate drive to create meaning and make sense of the world while faced with the impossibility of understanding the universe and our existence in its entirety.

*The Four Worlds
of Existence*

Step by step

1. The coach either asks the specific questions relating to each dimension (see above), or they listen to the client's narrative in response to an invitation to "tell me a bit about yourself".
2. The coach takes note of the significant aspects at each dimension, for further exploration later on.
3. If the client does not naturally reveal any information about their experience at any of these levels, the coach inquires with more specific questions relating to that respective world so as to arrive at a more rounded picture of the client.

Diagram: the four worlds

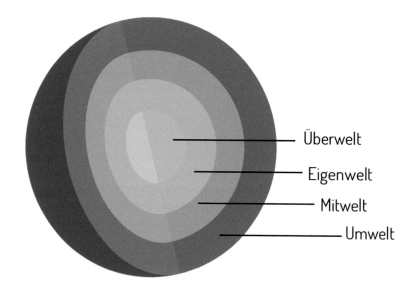

- Überwelt
- Eigenwelt
- Mitwelt
- Umwelt

References

Jacob, Y. (2019) *An Introduction to Existential Coaching*. London: Routledge.

van Deurzen, E. (2012) *Existential Counselling and Psychotherapy in Practice* (rev. 3rd edition). London: Sage Publications.

Yannick Jacob is an existential coach, positive psychologist, trainer, supervisor and Program Director of the Accredited Certificate in Integrative Coaching.

STOP

Ingredients

Phone, tablet or alarm

When does it work best?

The technique works best when clients complain that they find themselves caught up in a day of urgent tasks, or when they find themselves distracted by interesting tasks or emails, while neglecting important tasks. The task is best set as a homework or as an experiment to undertake outside of the coaching session. The use of a device reminder encourages a break and the process encourages the individual to refocus back on the priorities set at the start of the day.

Description

We live in turbulent times with immense change at both an individual level (as we need to learn and adapt to new technologies and processes) and at an organisational level (resulting from the forces of globalisation). Technological advances have created a new challenge for most managers working in organisations. While enhanced communication and access to information offer huge opportunities for efficiency, the flood of such information can become a drain on our time and mental resources. It's not unusual to find after a day of meetings that there are two hundred emails requiring responses. This short technique can help clients more effectively manage this balancing act by encouraging them to add in stop points during their day to review and re-plan the day's priorities, thus preventing them being drawn into the urgent, when they should be focused on the important.

Step by step

1. Describe the following approach to the client and invite them to try it daily as an experiment, between the current and the next session.
2. Set a trigger or reminder on a device. This can be for any time of day, although mid-morning and mid-afternoon work well.
3. Invite the client to stop what they are doing and be still for 30 seconds. Invite them to take a few conscious breaths, observing their in-breaths and out-breaths.
4. Ask the client to notice what they are doing. "How are you feeling? Are you doing what you need to be doing?"
5. Next, invite them to consider their options: "What options do you have to make a change? What do you need to change to achieve your priorities for the day?"
6. Finally, invite the client to refocus towards the important task of the day.

Reference

Passmore, J. (2017) Mindfulness Coaching Techniques: STOP. *The Coaching Psychologist*, 13(2), 86–7.

Jonathan Passmore is a chartered psychologist, accredited coach, supervisor and director of the Henley Centre for Coaching, Henley Business School.

Inner Mentor or Future Self

Ingredients

A quiet space

When does it work best?

This tool is good to use when the client is struggling in their current situation, due to insecurity, feeling unfulfilled and so forth. It can be very useful as a complement to the tools for working with the inner critic.

Description

This tool uses visualisation, which is a vehicle to see things differently by using one's imagination and by distancing oneself from the current reality (Passmore, 2020). Every person will experience this in a different way and in some cases, they may even be surprised by what they see. The images, feelings and thoughts they have during this visualisation can guide them when at a crossroads; they can ask themselves, "what would my future self (the one I saw that I like) do?" And then try to base their decisions on who they want to become and not who they currently are.

Step by step

1. Ask the client if they have thought of their future self. Do they want to do a visualisation that can help them connect with what they want in the future?
2. Invite the client to close their eyes, if they are comfortable doing so, to get in a comfortable position, to take some deep breaths and relax. A guided breathing exercise can help with achieving a relaxed state.
3. Walk the client through the following visualisation, pausing to give them time to take it in: "Imagine you are on earth, and you see a beam of light similar to a rainbow that goes up and up above the clouds. What colour is it? Get on it. This beam takes you up above the clouds, up into space, where everything is black, you see the sun burning bright in the distance. Then you see another beam of light of a different colour, and you follow it. This beam takes you away 20 years from now. It takes you down into earth, you go through the clouds, and down into a house to visit yourself 20 years in the future. Notice what kind of place this person lives in. Look around you, take in all the details. Find the door and now knock on it. Your future self will open the door. What is your future self doing? How is their presence, their look? When you go in the house, take in all the details: what is the decoration like? Your future self invites you to sit down in their favourite spot of the house and brings you a drink and some food."
4. Invite the client to chat with this older self, to ask them questions like "What has mattered most to you in the past 20 years?" The answer may come in any way: words, writing, a look, a gesture, a certain feeling that they give you. You can also ask them "What do I need to know to get from where I am to where you are?" Ask them any other question you feel like asking. If you have a dilemma in your lives, ask them about it, to see if there is something they want to say. Ask them how they would like for you to think about them. What can be their nickname?
5. As this conversation with a future self is coming to a close, invite the client to think about a future gift: "Your future self says they have a gift for

*Inner Mentor or
Future Self*

you, and they go to get it. Receive this present, and hold it tight for your journey back."

6. Help the client to return to now: "Now you see the beam of light you came in appear again. You follow it all the way into space, and you see again the original beam there waiting for you. You hop on the other beam of light and come back through the clouds to earth, to your current house. Take a deep breath and, whenever you are ready, open your eyes" (Mohr, 2015).

7. Invite the client to write down anything that comes to mind, giving them 5–6 minutes to write.

8. Invite them to share. Suggest some additional questions that they can write answers to (or that they can talk through), such as:
   a. What are you doing in your life right now that is inconsistent with the person, deep in your heart, that you truly want to be?
   b. What would you like to do differently?
   c. Does what you saw impact a relationship? Which one would you want it to be? What would you like to do differently?
   d. What have you learnt about yourself?
   e. How are you feeling?
   f. Are there any actions you want to take or anything you want to commit to?

References

Mohr, T., (2015) *Playing Big*. London: Arrow Books

Passmore, J. (Ed.), 2020. *The coaches' handbook: the complete practitioner guide for professional coaches*. New York: Routledge

Claudia Day is an accredited coach and entrepreneur with a marketing strategy background, and trained in coaching at Henley Business School and management at MIT Sloan.

Daydream Journal

Ingredients

Client notebook or paper and pen

When does it work best?

The technique can provide useful material about client values, beliefs and dreams that the coach can draw upon as material in future sessions.

Description

Research has revealed that most humans spend between 30% and 50% of their working day daydreaming (Killingsworth and Gilbert, 2010). It might be argued that daydreaming is the mind's default position. How can we use this information in coaching conversations? Daydreams provide useful insight into individuals' psychological constructs, particularly their hopes for the future, their values and priorities. We can use this material in coaching by inviting clients to capture their dreams through journaling.

Step by step

1. Invite the client to create a reflective journal and to spend some time each day capturing their thoughts. Some people will feel more comfortable writing notes, others capturing an audio diary.
2. The client should capture thoughts for more than one week, to allow patterns to emerge.
3. Ask the client to share this information with you prior to the next session, and review the journal or recordings.
4. Reflect on what these tell us about the client's aspirations for the future. What insights do they give as to their values, attitudes and current priorities?
5. Explore these aspects with your client in the next session.

Reference

Killingsworth, M., and Gilbert, D. (2010) A Wandering Mind is an Unhappy Mind. *Science*, 330, 932. DOI: 10.1126/ science.1192439

Eversley Felix is an executive coach and tutor on the Henley coaching programmes.

SHIFT

Ingredients

Short, bullet-point summary of differences between systems thinking and analytical thinking

Client notebook or reflective journal

Description

SHIFT was developed as a framework to support leaders seeking to enhance their strategic thinking and adapt their mindset when facing complex challenges. The SHIFT framework is influenced by systems thinking, transformational coaching perspectives on the value of purpose, and the theory of the triune brain (Maclean, 1990). The framework has been deployed successfully in FTSE 100 companies, in 2020.

SHIFT stands for:

- **Systems thinking** – SHIFT seeks to help clients develop from a simple cause-and-effect perspective to uncover the web of interconnected variables and dependencies behind many of their challenges.
- **Helpful approach** – SHIFT is designed to help clients draw motivation from their purpose and identify the unique way they can be helpful.
- **Intuition** – SHIFT seeks to enable clients to embrace a sense of self beyond cognition, connecting them with the reptilian (intuition), mammalian (feeling) and neo-cortex (thinking) elements of their brain.
- **Feeling** – SHIFT enables clients to connect with their feelings.
- **Thinking** – SHIFT encourages clients to embrace multiple thinking perspectives.

When does it work best?

The SHIFT framework is a useful tool for clients when the challenges they face are systemic and traditional analytical thinking approaches are insufficient. It can motivate clients, enabling them to connect with their purpose and the unique way they can be helpful and have impact. It can also support clients, helping them to move beyond a narrow cognitive perspective to a more holistic approach, connecting with the reptilian, mammalian and neo-cortex elements of their brain.

Step by step

1. Share the SHIFT framework with the client.
2. Systems thinking:
   a. Explain the difference between systems thinking and analytical thinking.
   b. Share tangible tools for thinking systemically – for example, the Cynefin Framework (Snowden and Boone, 2007).

SHIFT

c. Invite the client to consider which tools they are initially drawn to and to try out two or three before the next session, keeping a log of their experiences: When did they use it? What was its impact?

3. Helpful approach:
   a. Ask the client to spend five minutes reflecting on the following questions: Who does your team serve? What are your unique talents? How can you use these unique talents more effectively? What's holding you back?
   b. Invite the client to share their reflections and the one thing they can do next to begin activating them.

4. Integrating intuition, feeling and thinking:
   a. Share a range of techniques for accessing the best possible intuitive, feeling and thinking states. For the intuitive mode, this may be about moving from 'flight or fight' to presence, and potential techniques include exercise, mindful breathing and power poses. For the feeling mode, it may be about moving from self-centred emotion to socially focused emotion, and potential tools could be random acts of kindness or the metta-bhavana meditation. For the thinking mode, it may be about moving from clinical thinking to multiple perspectives, and potential tools may be reframing or pausing between stimulus and response.
   b. Invite the client to consider which tools they are initially drawn to, to try out one or two before the next session, and to log their experiences: When did they use it? What happened? What next?

5. In the next session, discuss the client's reflections about the SHIFT framework and their experience of the tools. Review their log and encourage them to keep the framework as a memorable acronym for mindset shifting and to use the tools which work best for them to enhance their thinking.

References

Maclean, P.D. (1990) *The Triune Brain: Role in Paleocerebral Functions*. New York: Springer.

Snowden, D.J., and Boone, M.E. (2007) A Leader's Framework for Decision Making. *Harvard Business Review*, 85(11): 68–76. Available from: https://hbr.org/2007/11/a-leaders-framework-for-decision-making

Matt Richards is an accredited ICF coach and prize-winning coaching master's graduate, and has led global companies for over 15 years.

Rebecca Palmer is an award-winning talent thought leader and coach specialising in bespoke solutions for FTSE 30 clients.

Decision-making Using Art

Ingredients

Any materials with which art can be created: pens, pencils, paint, collage, clay, etc.

Reference

Sheather, A. (2019) *Coaching Beyond Words: Using Art to Deepen and Enrich Our Conversations.* Abingdon: Routledge.

Claudia Day is an accredited coach and entrepreneur with a marketing strategy background, and trained in coaching at Henley Business School and management at MIT Sloan.

Description

Art has been a means of communication that humans have used since their early days, and it is thought to help us connect with a deeper part of ourselves, leading to greater insight. This is a guided exercise that helps the client explore a scenario that is relevant to their coaching aims. The process involves giving the client space so that images can emerge, using art to externalise their thinking. After going through the exercise, the coach can explore the meaning with the client through continuing with the coaching process (Sheather, 2019).

Step by step

1. Work with the client to help them define the available options as you would normally do.
2. Narrow down the options, again as you would usually do (ideally to three or four).
3. If the client is then finding it difficult to choose which option(s) to pursue, you can ask them if they want to try a painting/art exercise that may bring more awareness to them. Contract by explaining that:
   a. It would involve a visualisation and some art.
   b. It is not about creating a masterpiece, but about self-expression.
   c. It is a process of imaging, creating, connecting and exploring. They can explore as much as they want and stop at any point they wish.
   d. If they say yes, then move to step 4.
4. Invite them to close their eyes and breathe deeply three times for a mindful pause, to become fully present.
5. Then, staying in the mindfulness space, guide them through their options and allow images and feelings to come to the fore. You can accompany them through the journey by asking them questions that help them get more into the experience. For example: What can they see? Who is there? How does it feel?
6. Invite them to stay with the experience as long as they want, and once they have finished, to slowly come back to the room. They can:
   a. Open their eyes and capture in their artwork what they saw or felt in their mindful space, or what they feel now.
   b. Keep their eyes closed and capture in their artwork what they saw or felt in their mindful space, or what they feel now. They can then open their eyes and interpret the picture, based on their situation.
7. Once they finish, invite them to reflect on the experience.
8. When ready, close the exercise and continue the coaching.

AAA

Ingredients

Attitude: an open mind, willingness to reflect and a willingness to change

When does it work best?

This model works best when working one-to-one with a client who needs support in achieving personal change, but has yet to develop a clear internal dialogue or argument for making the change. This lack of internal argument, or justi-fication, reduces the motivation and thus contributes to the fizzling out of the change attempt, as described above.

Nicholas Lord is a human resources leader and executive coach. He is passionate about supporting change from both an individual and a business perspective.

Description

This model was initially designed to support the focus on diversity. I first developed it in South Africa at a time when the country, and its people, were going through a fundamental change and there was a burning need to embrace diversity and change mindsets.

The model assumes that all change starts with creating **awareness** (our first 'A'), either through creating or co-creating an understanding of the need for change and the importance of the change to the individual or group. This first step is usually explored well in a coaching session between coaches and individuals.

However, often we try to move straight from this new understanding to exploring the ways we can adapt to achieve the change. Too often, a step is missed. How many times have we created awareness, the client (or team) have said "great idea", then we immediately go about **adapting** (the third 'A') our processes, ways of working, changing our schedules and so on. And then the change fizzles out or, even worse, nothing happens?

This approach leaves out a crucial step: **acceptance** (the second 'A'). We can show a desire to change, but if we do not accept the need to change, this can often lead to failure.

Step by step

1. **A**wareness (creating awareness of the need to change): focus on the goal with the aim to explore not just the goal itself but also the feelings, assumptions and beliefs associated with it.
   1. Clarify the goal.
   2. Understand the drivers, feelings, assumptions and beliefs underlying it (the Five Whys approach works effectively here).
2. **A**cceptance (creating the acceptance that change is necessary and creating the buy-in to actually change): challenge and develop the client's growth mindset. This step is to get the client to truly own the change:
   1. Relate the change to the client's true desire to change (challenge-based questions work effectively here).
   2. Gain the client's commitment to the change.
3. **A**daptation (changing our mindsets, ways of working and assumptions to implement the change):
   1. Define what changes are needed, not only to implement the change, but to sustain it.
   2. Define the blockers and accelerators of the change.
   3. Reconfirm personal ownership.

The Ladder of Abstraction

Ingredients

Flipchart or whiteboard

Pens

Post-it notes

Description

The Ladder of Abstraction is a tool used in creative problem-solving to help frame a problem or question at the most useful level and to drive the generation and exploration of options and ideas. The Ladder is based on the principle that a problem needs to be asked at the right 'level' in order to come up with the most useful solutions. Using the analogy of a ladder, when you are on the higher rungs you are likely to be able to see the bigger picture and, when you are lower down, you will have greater detail. Both those perspectives are needed in order to address many complex issues. The Ladder uses the questions 'why?' (moving up the ladder) and 'how?' (moving down) to help a client explore what is driving a problem, determine how best to frame it and generate ideas at the most helpful level to address it (Isaksen et al., 2010).

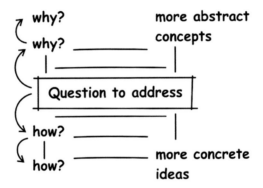

When does it work best?

The Ladder of Abstraction works well for both individuals and teams when a client is working on a complex problem that they are finding difficult to define (for instance, it may have multiple root causes and many possible solutions). It is a visual tool and enables clients to see links between issues and gain insight on how the framing of a problem can impact on how fully and appropriately it is ultimately addressed.

By encouraging the creative generation of ideas and the exploration of root causes, the Ladder can work very well as a group problem-solving tool. It enables exploration at both a strategic and a more operational level. A tool called a strategy map uses similar principles.

The Ladder of Abstraction

Step by step

1. Identify a problem question beginning with 'how to...?' Write it on a sticky note and put it on the wall or on a large piece of paper.
2. Ask the client to identify all the reasons they can think of for why this question should be addressed. These should be listed on separate sticky notes and added to the level above the original question.
3. It may be useful to continue up another 'rung' or two, asking 'why?' each time, to determine the root causes of the problem/question.
4. Throughout this exercise, encourage the client to reflect on the question: at what level would it be most useful to address the problem?
5. Use 'how?' questions to prompt the client to generate ideas for how specific problems identified in the 'why?' levels can be addressed (again, going down a number of rungs if it makes sense to do so).
6. The client should be encouraged to generate 'how?' ideas freely and creatively before considering the different options in greater detail.
7. Encourage the client to identify where they would like to focus their next efforts in addressing the problem question, at the level at which they have framed it.

References

Isaksen, S. Dorval, K. B. and Treffinger, D. (2010) *Creative Approaches to Problem Solving; A Framework for Innovation and Change* (3rd Edition). Sage.

Julie Flower is a leadership and team development coach, consultant and facilitator, specialising in navigating uncertainty in complex systems and applied improvisation.

Constellations

Ingredients

Wooden pawns in different colours and sizes, and in large numbers (e.g. 30+)

Or other small objects (e.g. shells, pebbles or Lego figures)

Sheet of A4 paper

Description

Every challenge we face is part of a system. Imagine if we could help unlock a situation by generating a perspective that is different to the one that we usually see. By creating a living map of a challenge and thus giving an x-ray view of the dynamics at play, we can help untangle a situation, bringing fresh clarity and new solutions. The constellations process was developed by Bert Hellinger, a German psychotherapist, originally for use in family systems (Hellinger, 2003). The techniques can be used successfully in coaching with individuals and teams. Using a variety of small props (Lego figures, sweets, chess pieces, pebbles, shells), the client creates a spatial representation of their current situation by mapping it out using a prop to represent each person or player, and positioning them accordingly on the map. Through a series of questions, the client explores the situation and the dynamics within it, then works on what needs to change by physically moving the props to new positions to create a breakthrough in thinking.

When does it work best?

This technique works best when a client has a block or feels stuck in the context of a specific scenario involving multiple people/players. The method brings a new perspective and energy through a non-verbal format, so it is ideal in situations where a client appears to be going round in circles, where you may sense there is information missing or where there seems to be a pattern of conflict around a topic. It works well for those who are less able to articulate what they want to communicate with words, as well as being effective in team coaching where each individual can map out their view of the situation, providing an opportunity to explore and understand different perspectives and look for common ground.

Step by step

1. You will need a blank A4 piece of paper and a selection of about 20–30 small props (e.g. Lego figures, small sweets, small pebbles). A varied selection is essential and they must be small enough for 10–12 of them to fit on the paper. If you're doing this virtually, brief the client in advance to prepare paper and a selection of objects. Alternatively, you can do this spontaneously using cups, Post-its, pens or whatever is to hand, and a tabletop. Or even leaves, twigs and stones if you are outdoors.
2. At the start of the session, give an overview of the approach, explaining the aim of creating a visual representation or living map of the topic or challenge that will enable a step back from it and a new perspective.

Constellations

3. Ask the client to give a brief description of the challenge they want to explore. Useful questions here are:
    - If this challenge were resolved, what would change for you?
    - If you were to create a map of the challenge, what elements would you need to include?
4. Place the sheet of paper in front of you and the client. If working virtually, the client should place the paper in front of them, and ideally as coach you should be able to see both the paper and the client.
5. Explain that the client will select 'representatives' using the objects, the objects themselves representing each person or element in the situation. The client should work intuitively, responding to the questions and selecting the objects freely, placing these anywhere, on or off the paper.
6. Ask the client to select their first representative and place it in a position that feels right to them. It is important that the client picks up and places each object themselves. As they select and then place the object, encourage them to talk out loud about their thinking and feelings. Do not push, though. Read and respect the client's willingness to share their process. For some, this can become a quiet, relatively private exercise, and the action itself can create an a-ha moment.
7. Encourage the client to think about where the representative needs to be placed. Where on the paper? Which direction should they be facing? What does the size, shape, colour of the object they chose tell them?
8. Ask the client what else should be on the map. Ask them again to select a representative and place it where it should be located. As they select and place the object, encourage them again to talk out loud about their thinking and feelings. Where does the representative need to be placed, especially in relation to the other objects? Is the distance between them right? How near or far should they be? What direction should they be facing? What do the size, shape and colour of the object they chose tell them? Explain that they can move any of the objects as they go. What is important is that it really represents their situation and feels right for them.
9. Continue asking the client what else needs to be included and work through the same process for each representative. Keep encouraging the client to talk through their thinking and feelings.
10. When the mapping is complete and all the representatives are in place, ask the client to take another look. Ask them: What is missing? Is anything else important here? Should someone or something else be considered at this stage?
11. Once the map is complete, encourage the client to step back and consider the map they have created, specifically exploring:
    - Representative objects (what drew them to that object?)
    - Time (the order the objects were placed on the paper)
    - Place (the distance between objects; the direction they face; what is on the paper and what is off the paper) and
    - Perspective (move around the map, look from different positions: what changes as you move position?).

Constellations

12. Explore what the exercise has highlighted for the client. Useful questions here include:
    - What story is the map telling you?
    - What has been brought to light that you didn't see before?
    - What new information do you have by looking at the situation in this way?
13. Now explore with the client what can be changed in the situation. Ask them to physically move representatives around, and talk through what they are doing and what the implications are for the situation. Useful questions here include:
    - What could be changed on your map to move one step towards a better situation?
    - Select one of the items on your map and see if you can move it to another location. What has changed?
    - What does this new map tell you?
14. Close the session by asking the client to reflect on the new insight they have gained, and what their actions will be moving forwards.

References

Hellinger, B. (2003) *Farewell: Family Constellations with Descendants of Victims and Perpetrators* (C. Beaumont, Trans.). Heidelberg, Germany: Carl-Auer-Systeme Verlag.

Whittington, J. (2016) *Systemic Coaching and Constellations: The Principles, Practices and Application for Individuals, Teams and Groups* (2nd edition). Kogan Page.

Claire Finch is a highly intuitive coach who supports individuals and teams to believe in themselves by unlocking their energy, so they can achieve their business and personal potential.

DARN CAT – Developing Change Talk

Ingredients

Client notebook or paper and pen

When does it work best?

The technique can be used to help coaches guide their listening and to prevent them closing a conversation too quickly, allowing clients instead to explore their ambivalence and develop enhanced motivation.

Description

During most coaching conversations, clients use language that signals their desire to make a change and also language that signals a reluctance to change, recognising most change comes with costs as well as benefits. One aspect of effective coaching is helping clients explore this ambiguity and build their commitment to the change. This is the focus of DARN CAT. The technique is situated within Motivational Interviewing (Miller and Rollnick, 2002), specifically during the contemplation phase. During this period, the coach needs to listen for statements labelled 'DARNs'. It is these statements that reveal an interest in, and consideration of, change. However, the client lacks a firm commitment to making the change. Such statements might express the individual's personal desires about making a change, the ability to make the change, their reasons for making the change and the need to change. Examples of these are summarised in the table.

Table Examples of DARN and CAT Statements

Desire	"I really want to do Y."
Ability	"I think I could do Y if I really wanted to…"
Reason	"If they did X, then I think that would be enough and I would then do Y."
Need	"I really need to do Y, or… will happen."
Commitment	"… next week I will do Y."
Action	"I am really keen this time to make a success of it. I have thought about what went wrong last time and it's going to be different on Tuesday."
Taking steps	"… in advance of next Tuesday, I have already done X. This will mean that when the meeting comes on Tuesday, Y should be much easier this time."

In general terms, the coach should look out for statements that are conditional or hypothetical and encourage the client to continue to explore the situation. As a deeper understanding of the situation and the client's priorities emerges, the client's language will begin to change towards CAT talk, which includes **c**ommitments, **a**ctions and **t**aking first steps.

DARN CAT – Developing Change Talk

Step by step

1. Listen to the client's talk.
2. Note DARN statements, which may include **d**esire, **a**bility, **r**easons and **n**eed to change, and encourage the client to continue to talk.
3. Explore the client's values and long-term priorities.
4. Support the client and note any changes in language towards **c**ommitments, **a**ctions and **t**aking first steps.
5. As CAT talk emerges, support the client to crystalise their plans, and to recognise that change is challenging and that slips and relapses can occur – but they should not give up!

Reference

Miller, W., and Rollnick, S. (2002) *Motivational Interview: Preparing People for Change* (2nd edition). New York: Guildford Press.

Jonathan Passmore is a chartered psychologist, accredited coach, supervisor and director of the Henley Centre for Coaching, Henley Business School.

Storyboarding

Ingredients

Plain paper – enough for a storyboard of up to six frames (A3 works well)

Felt-tipped pens in a variety of colours

When does it work best?

A benefit of the use of storyboarding in coaching is the opportunity it offers for clients to *see* their topic from a different viewpoint. It is particularly useful when the client is undertaking detailed planning about a change. It helps to use the terms 'sketching' or 'doodling' rather than 'drawing', as the latter might cause an unhelpful 'I can't draw' response.

Description

Storyboards are used in the media to outline the main points of a narrative and to establish the directions, such as suggested camera angles, for turning the pictures on a page into a finished film. The client's storyboard can comprise as many frames as are needed; however, six frames are a typical maximum. The first frame comprises a sketch of the current nature of the client's chosen topic, and the final frame depicts the desired scenario. The frames between the present and future states represent the principal milestones and critical success factors for ensuring the end result is achieved.

An example

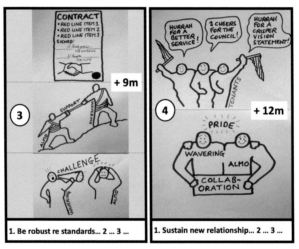

Storyboarding

Background (a storyboard reconstructed following a coaching session)

My client was a senior manager in a local authority with responsibility for housing services, which had been contracted out to an arms-length management organisation (ALMO). The ALMO was independent from the council, which had representation on its board, and was providing a poor-quality service. Tenants were unclear about the management arrangements and so were targeting their complaints at the council, which was bearing the brunt of the very negative press coverage and was 'wavering' in its response. My client used storyboarding to explore the relationship between the council and the ALMO, and decided that robust challenge alongside a stronger collaborative approach would be the most effective way forward. The conversation around the storyboard enabled the implications of the client's (negative and positive) feelings about the situation to be explored, leading to the humour included in the sketches – which, it transpired, had some important and serious underpinnings.

Picture source: David Love

Step by step

1. Help your client decide where to start – the present situation (the first frame) or the desired future state (the last frame). Invite them to sketch the key elements of each of these positions in turn. Enable them to gain a detailed grasp of what is involved in both cases, by challenging constructively their assumptions and perceptions – not forgetting the impact of the emotional elements involved.
2. Establish a relevant timescale for the achievement of the future position and add this to the final frame sketch.
3. Encourage the client to establish an appropriate number of intervening frames and to focus on populating these – starting wherever the client chooses. Notice how they go about making their decisions.
4. Invite your client to produce sketches for the key elements that need to be included in each frame. Provide support and constructive challenge to enable the them to develop their understanding and insight. Encourage the client to give a running commentary about the creation of the storyboard.
5. Ask the client to allocate a date to each frame so that each one has a clear position in the overall timeline.
6. When all the frames have been sketched, turn the client's attention to the actions that are required to ensure each milestone is achieved. Invite the client to add captions beneath each frame to identify the two or three key actions required to make progress to the next frame.
7. Invite your client to review the insights and lessons learnt from the story-board – and from the process of producing it.

References

Gash, J. (2017) Visual Processes. In *Coaching Creativity – Transforming Your Practice*. Abingdon: Routledge, Part V, Chapter 18, pp.155–66.

Sibbert, D. (2013) *Visual Leaders – New Tools for Visioning, Management and Organization Change*. The Grove Consultants International, pp.18 and 147 (Story-mapping).

David Love is an executive coach and supervisor, working with public service leaders. He also teaches on Henley Business School's coaching programme.

ABCDEF Model

Ingredients

Pen and paper

Table with six columns, headed 'A', 'B', 'C', 'D', 'E' and 'F'

Description

In Cognitive Behavioural Therapy (CBT), the ABCDEF model is drawn and adapted from the research of Ellis (1962) and Beck (1976). It has been applied to Cognitive Behavioural Coaching (CBC) along with a number of other tools (Neenan, 2008). Michael Neenan describes the ABC tool as "the centrepiece of CBC practice" (2008: 3). The six letters stand for: **a**ntecedent (or **a**wareness), **b**eliefs (and thoughts), **c**onsequences (emotions and behaviours), **d**isputation, **e**ffective learning and **f**eelings (and **f**uture).

When does it work best?

The ABCDEF model is used as an effective coaching tool to encourage a client to re-evaluate their negative automatic thoughts (NATs). These are unhelpful, assumptive and/or distortive thoughts, images and beliefs, which are often referred to in CBC as 'thinking errors'. For example: *polarised thinking*, also referred to as 'black and white' or 'all or nothing' thinking; *mind-reading*, whereby we assume to know the thoughts and intentions of others; *catastrophising*, where we maximise the importance of negative events and minimise the importance of positive events; *overgeneralising*, where we may see a single unpleasant event as evidence that either everything is terrible or will prove to go wrong. This is not to say that the client's thoughts and beliefs are always incorrect and must therefore be modified; in fact, it is only if they have a negative effect that the coaching sessions can then focus on accepting and/or managing those thoughts to the point where they allow the client to achieve their goal.

Step by step

1. In the coaching session, explain the model to the client and why you've identified from the issue that ABCDEF may be relevant.
2. The client should divide their paper into six columns, headed 'A', 'B', 'C', 'D', 'E' and 'F'.
3. Invite the client to bring into their present awareness a previous experience (**a**ntecedent) that triggered unhelpful emotions and behaviours (**c**onsequences) because of certain thoughts or **b**eliefs held by the client. This can be captured by asking the client to write down a challenge statement. For example: *"I felt embarrassed, upset and frustrated* [consequences] *when my manager asked our group for ideas but didn't specifically ask for my input* [antecedent]. *I believe this is because she doesn't think much of my opinion* [belief]. *Consequently, it led me to disengage from the meeting* [consequences]." The coach then helps the client break down their challenge statement into its ABC elements in the following steps.

ABCDEF Model

4. Write down the awareness of the antecedent (a singular event) in column A and the associated unhelpful emotional and behavioural consequences in column C.
5. Now invite the client to list in column B the beliefs and thoughts that went through their mind when the antecedent event presented itself.
6. Next, the client is invited to presently reflect and dispute the logic or reality of such beliefs and/or thoughts (**d**isputation) listed in column B. For example, given the context, does B fit with reality? Does it seem reasonable and logical? Is B generally helpful, and does it catalyse positive relationships and the attainment of constructive and reasonable goals?
7. Once your client has ascertained and processed those emotionally charged thoughts and beliefs that they associate with the event or situation (antecedent), the client can then form and write down an *alternative* line of thinking that is based upon thoughts and beliefs that may be more logical, reasonable, helpful and constructive.
8. In column F, the client is invited to change their aforementioned challenge statement to a goal statement, so as to now focus on a future goal that includes helpful consequences. For example: *"When I am in a meeting and am not directly asked for my input* [awareness or antecedent], *I want to maintain my engagement by contributing at appropriate times* [consequences – behaviours] *while feeling calm, confident and empathetic to the group's needs* [consequences – emotions]."
9. The client is asked how they will measure the successful execution of this goal.
10. Finally, the client is asked to explore how they feel about this goal statement and this process, and if there is anything else that they would like to stop, start or continue in order to ensure the future success of their goal.

References

Beck, A.T. (1976) *Cognitive Therapy and the Emotional Disorders.* Oxford: International Universities Press.

Ellis, A. (1962) *Reason and Emotion in Psychotherapy.* Oxford: Lyle Stuart.

Neenan, M. (2008) From Cognitive Behaviour Therapy (CBT) to Cognitive Behaviour Coaching (CBC). *Journal of Rational-Emotive & Cognitive-Behavior Therapy*, 26(1): 3–15. doi:10.1007/s10942-007-0073-2

Callum O'Neill is a Henley coach specialising in executive, team and systems coaching, with a particular interest in double and triple loop learning.

Seventh-generation Thinking

Ingredients

A personal story to illustrate stewardship

Description

In complex systems, there are always time delays between the decision or action and ongoing consequences of that decision. For example, when my mother passed away, I planted a scented rose, called 'Remember Me', in her favourite colour. It is still only a foot high, but as a climbing rose it will grow and spread. In the years to come, her grandchildren will be able to remember her as they sit alongside the scented, brightly coloured roses. In a further 20 years, their children may play and collect the petals from the roses to make potpourri bunches and carry the fragrance back to their own homes. Many years in the future, many future generations will enjoy the beauty and scent of these roses, entwined in the branches of a tree and decorating the view across the neighbourhood with their colour. Of course, it need not be a rose we plant, but a single beech tree or a wood. The Iroquois nation of North America recognised the long shadows our decisions cast, calling this 'Seventh-generation stewardship'. This tool seeks to help our clients integrate long-term decision-making into their organisational decision-making processes, both for daily actions and strategic decisions. Seventh-generation thinking urges current leaders to live and work for the benefit of the seventh generation into the future. As the Iroquois people said: *"In all of your deliberations… look and listen for the welfare of the whole people and have always in view not only the past and present but also the coming generations, even those whose faces are yet beneath the surface of the ground – the unborn of the future"*.

Step by step

1. Share a personal story to illustrate seventh-generational thinking and link this to the sayings of the Iroquois nation.
2. Invite the client to explore a strategy decision being considered by the board.
3. Explore this through multiple future generations: Who benefits? How much? Who bears the costs? When will the costs be felt? How long do these costs last?
4. Invite the client, as in a SWOT analysis, to map the results.

Jacqui Zanetti is an executive coach with a corporate background and a strong interest in international leadership.

The Time to Think Council

Ingredients

Pen and paper

When does it work best?

This can be a useful team coaching tool when a group of people have diverse views, but it requires the group to have contracted around how they will work together, and a willingness to listen and to seek to understand. It is also good when you have a group of people who are going through a similar situation and can support each other through this process.

Description

This tool was devised by Nancy Kline and Scott Farnsworth (Kline, 2015) and draws on Kline's Time to Think approach (Kline, 1999). The aim is for a person to benefit from the wisdom of a group while still thinking independently. One person at a time decides a topic, and all others provide uninterrupted, appreciative attention and then respond to a question posed by the person without giving advice (avoid phrases such as 'I think you should' or 'if I were you, I would').

Step by step

The group will alternate the roles.

1. Presenter: identifies the issue or dilemma, and thinks out loud about it for ten minutes. Then thinks of a question they would like people to answer.
2. Scribe: records on paper what each says.
3. Facilitator: confirms the question, and asks for clarifying questions.
4. Everybody: speaks from their experience or on something that came up for them, such as an object in their room, a metaphor, a song, poem, a quote or other information, using phrases like: 'I have found that in my experience', 'once, the following thing happened to me' or 'if I were facing that situation, I would'.
5. Presenter: says final thoughts while group listens.
6. Everybody: says a quality they admire in the presenter.

Reference

Kline, N. (1999) *Time to Think*. London: Cassell.

Kline, N. (2015) *More Time to Think*. London: Cassell.

Claudia Day is an accredited coach and entrepreneur with a marketing strategy background, and trained in coaching at Henley Business School and management at MIT Sloan.

Blessings: Cultivating a Compassionate Mind

Ingredients

Attitude: acceptance and love

When does it work best?

The technique is one that can be used by the coach, or taught to the client, as a means to develop a compassionate mind. It can be used at any, or all times, for we can never have too much love for our passengers on this journey through life.

Reference

Passmore, J. (2020) *The coaches' handbook: the complete practitioner guide for professional coaches*. New York: Routledge

Jonathan Passmore is a chartered psychologist, accredited coach, supervisor and director of the Henley Centre for Coaching, Henley Business School.

Description

This technique is useful for cultivating a compassionate mind. It can be used by the coach or client (Passmore, 2020) and is a perfect antidote to feelings of anxiety, stress or boredom, when travelling with others, either on public transport or when stuck in busy traffic. As we look around us, we can see composed faces; faces that reveal nothing. But one person may be worried about their teenage daughter, another dreaming about their new lover, a third sad about their boring job, while a fourth may be fearful of what their predatory boss may do next. We never know what is behind each façade, but we can try to empathise with the multiple feelings of humanity – sadness, joy, fear – and offer each person a blessing for their day: "May your day be blessed, and you carry with you joy and peace in your heart to the next people you meet." Occasionally, just occasionally, someone will look up and catch our eye. In these situations, we can offer a warm smile. Most times, the person smiles back, and sometimes nods, while all around, our fellow travellers are trying hard to pretend they are alone. Maybe this tiny interaction brightens the other person's day. These shared moments of loving kindness can also brighten our day. They remind us that, while we are one of eight billion people on this planet, each of them is just like us, trying their best to earn a living for their family and live a peaceful, happy and fulfilled life. While this technique won't change the world, it may gradually change you.

Step by step

1. Introduce the idea to the client by sharing a story.
2. Invite the client, next time they are on a bus, tube or train, or stuck in a traffic jam, to start with the person next to them. The client should look at them and imagine what might be happening for them. Silently, in their own mind, the client should offer them a gentle and loving blessing, and then move on to the next person and repeat the process.
3. If someone looks up, offer them a warm smile.

And finally…

May this book bring you blessings as you continue your journey as a coach and engage in the practices shared by this community.

The danger of using tools

While this book focuses exclusively on tools, we don't want you to assume tools are the end-all and be-all of coaching. In fact, we believe it's quite the reverse. Coaching is essentially a relationship between two people. In Carl Rogers' language, one, the coach, is congruent within the relationship; the other, the client, brings incongruence, in the form of an issue, a problem or a topic to explore. Of course, in reality, we are all incongruent. We all have dilemmas, troubles, anxieties or emotions. This congruence–incongruence relationship means that, unlike a 'normal conversation' between friends, which moves back and forward between their respective interests or concerns, in coaching, all the focus is towards the interests or concerns of the client

This unique feature of coaching means that the coach needs to bring with them a high level of skill in managing the process, thus enabling the client to remain focused on their content. Effective coaches are able to draw on advanced inter-personal skills – listening, summarising, reflecting, affirming, using silence and questions – to help the client navigate their way through the process and emerge with new insights, plans and personal learning. It is these skills that are the basic ingredients of effective coaching. Only once these basic skills have been mastered should the coach turn to tools to assist in the exploration and navigation of the journey.

When offered a 'cookbook of tools', there are a host of dangers lying ahead for the novice coach presented with such an array. We would advocate being mindful of potential pitfalls, which can help the coach stay focused on the core ingredients and keep in mind that tools are but the cherries on the cake.

So, here are five dangers of coaching tools:

1. **'The law of the instrument':** one of the biggest dangers is the coach who has a tool and uses it in every situation. 'Maslow's Hammer', as this dilemma is known, is a common challenge for us all. We may be highly skilled in using a particularly tool, but the question is: is it the right tool for this client, for this issue, or at this moment in the conversation? Our view is that by creating a massive toolbox, coaches can expand their repertoire and thus have 50 or 100 tools in their toolkit, not just five or ten.

2. **Coaching tools beat listening:** a second danger is a belief that tools can always get us out of a situation. Instead, we would argue that returning to listening and reflecting back is almost always more powerful than a tool. Tools are an amazing resource, but only when combined with the core coaching skills.

The danger of
using tools

3. **The magic of the tool:** a third danger of tools is the way they are intro-duced. Some coaches might be tempted to suggest to clients that the tool is a form of magic or creates a transformational moment. While new insights can emerge from their use, we would advocate lowering client expectations. One way to do this is using the word 'experiment': "Would you be happy to try an experiment? We have found that some clients sometimes find this helpful." This allows the client to find it *not* helpful, and thus for the 'experiment' to fail. Nothing is lost, and the coach and client can continue on their journey.

4. **I have never done it before:** the fourth danger is experimenting with a new tool on paying clients. We would advocate that you find ways to practise the first two or three times with peers (for example, on a course) or when providing pro-bono coaching, but making it clear in your contracting that you will be trying out new tools and approaches you may not have used before. This allows you to develop the 'script' to introduce the tool and get a sense of how it lands with different clients before you start using it with paying clients.

5. **'Look how clever I am':** the final danger is that the tool becomes a 'party piece', which the coach believes demonstrates to the client just how wonderful they are. This is most likely to happen when the coach focuses on their signature tools. We would suggest being a Jack or Jill of all trades, capable of using many tools, and using the one that you believe is best for your client and their specific situation.

Categorisation: using the tools in different coaching situations

The tools in this book cover a diverse range of topics and can be used in a wide range of coaching situations. We have put together a simple index of tools that you might find useful to support clients with certain presenting topics.

These categories are by no means exhaustive and the allocation of different tools to different categories is based purely on our editorial judgement. However, if you are stuck for inspiration or would like to explore a range of approaches for supporting clients with particular issues then this index may be helpful for you.

Behavioural change: *p. 12, 21, 42, 49, 51, 55, 61, 63, 64, 104, 110, 112, 114, 119, 132, 153, 159, 166, 172*

Career: *p. 17, 47, 68, 86, 98, 113, 124*

Clarifying thinking: *p. 10, 17, 19, 25, 26, 35, 53, 74, 75, 82, 88, 94, 118, 129, 133, 148, 154, 167, 174, 176, 180*

Confidence: *p. 8, 10, 23, 28, 34, 54, 65, 78, 92, 116, 119, 132, 133*

Creative thinking: *p. 5, 26, 28, 32, 53, 66, 68, 82, 126, 147, 152, 165, 167, 169*

Decision-making: *p. 10, 14, 17, 25, 34, 51, 84, 88, 129, 139, 147, 148, 154, 155, 165, 172, 178*

Disrupting patterns: *p. 5, 23, 31, 35, 42, 82, 94, 96, 104, 108, 126, 130, 143, 146, 152, 153, 159*

Emotions: *p. 23, 54, 61, 75, 135, 140, 176*

Experimentation: *p. 5*

Goal-setting: *p. 26, 49, 55, 63, 110, 119, 120, 128, 142*

Group coaching: *p. 6, 180*

Leadership: *p. 21, 49, 71, 105, 106, 113, 140, 163, 178*

Limiting beliefs: *p. 31, 32, 65, 96, 108, 135, 160*

Meaning and purpose: *p. 19, 57, 70, 102, 124, 142, 148, 150, 155, 157, 163*

Options: *p. 5, 66, 118, 147, 152, 165, 167, 172*

Personal growth: *p. 34, 86, 90, 105, 150*

Perspective: *p. 8, 12, 25, 32, 35, 44, 57, 66, 68, 74, 75, 84, 88, 94, 105, 126, 130, 135, 139, 147, 167, 169, 174*

Planning change: *p. 10, 17, 21, 37, 51, 55, 57, 64, 71, 74, 86, 88, 92, 98, 110, 112, 123, 126, 129, 139, 165, 166, 172, 174, 178*

Prioritisation: *p. 14, 51, 112, 142, 154, 159*

Reaching potential: *p. 8, 19, 46, 86, 110, 113, 116, 118, 139, 142*

Reflection: *p. 42, 44, 53, 55, 61, 64, 65, 70, 74, 77, 90, 94, 124, 128, 143, 148, 150, 151, 153, 162, 180*

Relationships: *p. 6, 42, 44, 137, 140, 146, 162*